SHOPPING FOR PORCUPINE

SETH
KANTNER

SHOPPING FOR PORCUPINE

a life in arctic alaska

Milkweed Editions

Published 2008 by Milkweed Editions
Printed in Canada
Cover design by Christian Fuenfhausen
Front cover photo of Howard Kantner outside of igloo at Cape Thompson, 1961, by Austin Thomas
Author photo by China Kantner
Interior design by Linda McKnight
Interior photographs by Seth Kantner unless otherwise noted
The text of this book is set in Sabon and Gill Sans
08 09 10 11 12 5 4 3 2 1
First Edition

Special underwriting for this book was contributed by John and Joanne Gordon, in honor of their parents.

Milkweed Editions, a nonprofit publisher, gratefully acknowledges sustaining support from Anonymous; Emilie and Henry Buchwald; the Bush Foundation; the Patrick and Aimee Butler Family Foundation; CarVal Investors; the Dougherty Family Foundation; the Ecolab Foundation; the General Mills Foundation; the Claire Giannini Fund; John and Joanne Gordon; William and Jeanne Grandy; the Jerome Foundation; Dorothy Kaplan Light and Ernest Light; Constance B. Kunin; Marshall BankFirst Corp.; Sanders and Tasha Marvin; the May Department Stores Company Foundation; the McKnight Foundation; a grant from the Minnesota State Arts Board, through an appropriation by the Minnesota State Legislature, a grant from the National Endowment for the Arts, and private funders; an award from the National Endowment for the Arts, which believes that a great nation deserves great art; the Navarre Corporation; Debbie Reynolds; the Starbucks Foundation; the St. Paul Travelers Foundation; Ellen and Sheldon Sturgis; the Target Foundation; the Gertrude Sexton Thompson Charitable Trust (George R. A. Johnson, Trustee); the James R. Thorpe Foundation; the Toro Foundation; Moira and John Turner; United Parcel Service; Joanne and Phil Von Blon; Kathleen and Bill Wanner; Serene and Christopher Warren; the W. M. Foundation; and the Xcel Energy Foundation.

Library of Congress Cataloging-in-Publication Data
Kantner, Seth, 1965–
    Shopping for porcupine : a life in arctic Alaska / Seth Kantner. — 1st ed.
    p.   cm.
    ISBN 978-1-57131-301-0 (alk. paper)
    1. Kantner, Seth, 1965—Childhood and youth. 2. Authors, American—20th century— Biography.
3. Arctic regions—Biography. 4. Wilderness areas—Biography. 5. Conservation of natural resources—
Arctic regions. 6. Arctic peoples—Hunting. 7. Arctic regions—Social life and customs. 8. Alaska—
Biography. I. Title.
    PS3611.A55Z46 2008
    813'.6—dc22
    [B]
                                            2007046477

This book is printed on acid-free paper.

NATIONAL
ENDOWMENT
FOR THE ARTS

A great nation
deserves great art.

MINNESOTA
STATE ARTS BOARD

for my dad, who chose the tundra

contents

also by Seth Kantner
Ordinary Wolves

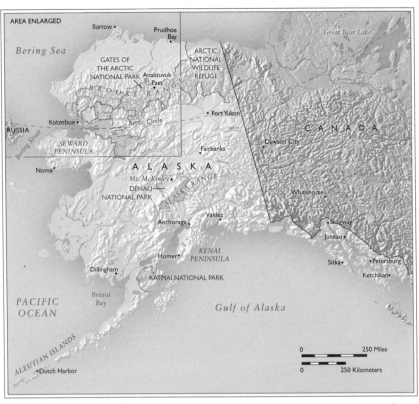

AREA ENLARGED

Bering Sea

Barrow •
Prudhoe Bay •

GATES OF THE ARCTIC NATIONAL PARK

Anaktuvuk Pass •

ARCTIC NATIONAL WILDLIFE REFUGE

B R O O K S   R A N G E

Great Bear Lake

• Fort Yukon

RUSSIA

Kotzebue •

Arctic Circle

SEWARD PENINSULA

Fairbanks •

A L A S K A

C A N A D A

• Dawson City

Nome •

Mt. McKinley ▲

DENALI NATIONAL PARK

A L A S K A   R A N G E

Whitehorse •

Anchorage •

Valdez •

• Skagway

Juneau •

Homer •

KENAI PENINSULA

Sitka •

• Petersburg

Dillingham •

KATMAI NATIONAL PARK

Ketchikan •

PACIFIC OCEAN

Bristol Bay

Gulf of Alaska

ALEUTIAN ISLANDS

• Dutch Harbor

0   250 Miles

0   250 Kilometers

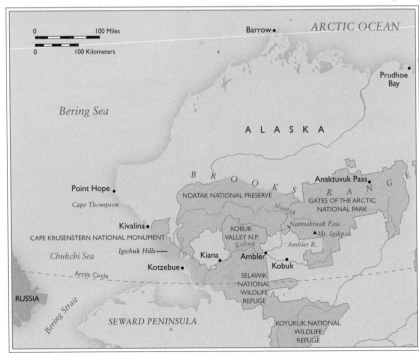

0   100 Miles

0   100 Kilometers

Barrow •

ARCTIC OCEAN

Prudhoe Bay •

Bering Sea

A L A S K A

B R O O K S

Anaktuvuk Pass •

R A N G E

Point Hope •

NOATAK NATIONAL PRESERVE

Cape Thompson

Noatak

GATES OF THE ARCTIC NATIONAL PARK

Kivalina •

CAPE KRUSENSTERN NATIONAL MONUMENT

Igichuk Hills —

Chukchi Sea

Kiana •

KOBUK VALLEY N.P.

Kobuk

Ambler •

Natmaktuak Pass

▲ Mt. Igikpak

Ambler R.

Kobuk •

Arctic Circle

Kotzebue •

SELAWIK NATIONAL WILDLIFE REFUGE

RUSSIA

Bering Strait

SEWARD PENINSULA

KOYUKUK NATIONAL WILDLIFE REFUGE

Erna Kantner on a dogsled with two-year-old Kole, 1965 (Photo by Howard Kantner)

aana	grandma
aqpik	salmonberry (aqpiks, modern usage plural)
aŋatkuq	shaman (aŋatkut, plural)
arii	hurt, disappointment (elder pronunciation)
ichuun	skin scraper, flensing tool
itchaurat	lacey intestinal fat
ittukpalak	whipped fish-egg and cranberry pudding
malik	follow, accompany
mamillak	waterproof mukluks (mamillaks, modern usage plural)
niqipiaq	Eskimo food
paniqtuq	dried meat
patiq	marrow
paatnaq	partner (slang)
pauṅġaq	crowberry (pauṅġaqs, modern usage plural)
qaatchiaq	skin mattress, traditionally caribou hide (qaatchiaqs, modern usage plural)
quaġaq	fermented sourdock
quaq	frozen meat or fish, often aged or fermented
qusrimmaq	wild rhubarb
suakataq	scold
tiktaaliq	mudshark
tinnik	bearberry
tuuq	ice chisel
ugruk	bearded seal
ulu	curved women's knife
umiaq	skin boat (umiat, plural)
umialik	whaling captain or boat captain
umiŋmak	muskoxen (umiŋmaich, plural)

SHOPPING FOR PORCUPINE

the candy store

Standing on the rocks in front of MacManuses' old sod igloo at Paun-gaqtaugruk bluff, I watch the current twist by and somehow I get to remembering Susan's imaginary candy store, of all things. The house is thirty-seven years old, overgrown, leaning and lonely. Notched posts recline; sagging ridge beams ride them imperceptibly down. Healthy young spruce and birch grow on the moss roof. Porcupine, mice, and marten have clawed out the homemade Visqueen windows and tun-neled through the sod-block and sapling walls to marble the floorboards with turds. Bears have walked in, bitten empty Clorox and syrup jugs, walked back out.

I was a four-and-a-half-year-old kid living two miles downriver when this place smelled fresh with the sap of split poles and peeled logs, overflowing with voices, the hiss of a Coleman lantern and the vigor of sweat and plans. Over the decades I've watched it coming down, mold-ing and slumping back to the ground, and I suspect it will take more than the rest of my life to disappear.

Across the Kobuk River, an ancient stand of spruce darkly guards the tundra beyond. That timber will always remind me of black bear meat—from a fragmented memory of a bear my dad and others shot in a tree—and of that candy store. Susan was five or six when they moved here and lived a couple seasons at this spot, thirty river miles below the village of Ambler. My family had lived down at the lower end of the bluff since before I was zero. We lived there because my dad respected, maybe more than all else, this land and the way the Eskimos used to live on it. I have no idea why the MacManuses came, but I believe the reasons were different.

Susan arrived with real powdered toothpaste, stories of exotic realms such as Seattle, and belongings. We brushed our teeth with salt and soda. Our stuff was mostly dog harnesses and caribou skins and dark brown tools with lighter brown handles. My dad's brass bread box, a Herter's fox call, and an RCBS reloader were about our shiniest show-off items, and my brother and I learned abruptly that fall that they weren't worth pointing out.

MacManuses had a three-foot-long oval galvanized washtub, with no leak. Two kids could take a bath at once. And they had a washing machine. The day I'm remembering, Susan's older brother, Scott, had the first rabbit he'd ever snared down in that gasoline-powered Maytag—still alive and occasionally screaming. Susan was supposed to be doing her correspondence-school work, but somehow she ended up leading me out across the river ice toward the dark spruce. Looking for the candy store, of course.

The thing I remember most painfully about the candy store was that you had to give Susan sweets for her to build up the generosity to lead you there. Then along the way, she'd stop. "If I had some candy"— she'd pause, and glance around—"I might be able to remember the trail. Don't worry, there'll be plenty when we get there." You had no

Dusk on the river:
Paungaqtaugruk
bluff along the
north shore

choice but to improve her memory with whatever you had. I rarely had anything in my pockets besides lint, string, and empty .22 shells. My mother was a health-food person and worried over our diet, so we were seldom allowed candy, not much sugar, and no pop.

I can't imagine my having candy that day, and I don't believe Susan operated on credit. But those were long winters in our small sod houses, with mice rustling in the walls and under the tables and foxes tunneling down to steal dog food; sled dogs being traded; paperbacks being borrowed back and forth and read down to tatters; and we kids too with our own heavy bartering going on. So actually Susan might have been willing to accept a promise.

Regardless, we ended up out on that river. My brother, Kole, wouldn't come along. He was cynical about the whole subject. He'd been stung pretty badly once when we did have candy. That particular time Susan had tried to convince him that the store had caught fire. This after she'd finished his Hershey's bar and nearly froze his kneecaps off searching. "Where are the burned logs?" he asked. Even then he was pragmatic. We'd grown up on the tundra, hauling things home to eat. We asked simple questions and wanted useful answers. Did something work, was it good to eat, did it hold a knot?

That day an east wind had the snow up and moving. The river was a quarter mile wide with deep drifts—miles across to a five- and six-year-old. We hunched close and protected our faces as best we could. Frostbite was a way of life back then. We called it "your face is white" and helped each other thaw out with our palms. Then we slid our mittens back on and continued. Cold was, well . . . just cold. Nobody wore these Darth Vader snowgo masks people use today. Back then along the Kobuk River if you were sissy enough to wear a mask like that people would have talked about you all the way to Kotzebue. *What them white people always try save their face for anyways?* is what folks would have said and thought.

Eventually, Susan and I made it to the far bank and there the snow had drifted even deeper. At that age I didn't wear extra stuff, like socks, or underwear. My mukluks filled up. We stood as uncertain as caribou, unwilling to start back. Our eyes crusted with ice. Susan patiently explained how the owners must have had to move the store because of the wind. It was plausible. By then the wind had increased and it was hard to make out the bluff on the north shore. And then all Susan's work pitching her vision of that candy store warm and heaped with sweets sort of blew away downstream. We headed back.

On the way we thought we heard a motor. We yanked off our scarves, pried open our hats and hoods, ignoring the gusting snow and cold, forgetting all about candy. There was almost nothing more important. A motor meant visitors, people; it might be Clarence Wood hunting on his Snow Traveler, as the first snowmobiles were called. Or it might be Harry Tickett with mail and packages from the post office, maybe Tony Bernhardt in his Super Cub, bounty-hunting wolves, bringing us ice cream bars and asking our parents when the wolf packs had last showed. When we heard a motor, at first, *who* didn't really matter. Anybody would at least be somebody. Maybe the people or person would spend the night. Probably they'd stop, say nothing to us kids, a little to the adults, have coffee, and go on. And even that would be a big deal.

But it was no motor—nor a traveler on his dog team like Don Williams who once a year might even play the guitar and sing—only the wind, which we had no scarcity of, and it seemed scarcity was how we measured value. We slogged back to the shore, up the drifts, past the dogs and the washing machine and inside the house. We stood red-faced, thawing out by the barrel stove. Scott's rabbit had met Scott's hammer and that was over, and Scott and Susan showed Kole and me what super-duper was: hot Tang with Eagle Brand sweetened condensed milk stirred in, and that too was a great novelty as our family didn't have either.

The candy store was never found, at least not when I was present. Along the years electricity came to Ambler and other villages, and flush toilets and the first community telephone, and then enough for people to have their own phones, their own color of phone. By then MacManuses had long moved upriver to the village and got jobs as schoolteachers. Susan grew beautiful, and she moved away where most stores have candy and she doesn't have to fish anymore for her family's dogs and start a campfire every night to cook dog pot in a third of a drum.

And now on the shore in front of the old place, I hear a boat coming. I don't feel any of that old excitement we once felt. It's nearly 2010. A lot of aluminum and fiberglass boats pass, looking for something to shoot. Although I'm not nearly an elder, sometimes it's tough, watching all these young people and newcomers rush past with their fast and fancy equipment, with little room on board for knowledge or respect for those by-hand times so recently passed.

Some of the old-timers are still alive, the ones like Nelson Greist, who walked from Point Barrow, and Minnie Gray, whose family seasonally lined their boat up the Kobuk, and others who remember the taste of famine, dark, and eating sealskin to survive. Things that we kids at Paungaqtaugruk never experienced. But that past of treasuring the simplest possessions and meals leaves us all uprooted at times in the face of such heaped and flippant wealth.

I'm thinking maybe we've found that mythical candy store after all. I should call Susan. Talking about our old days along this river would peel all that away. We would laugh a lot. And I guess I better find out if she still has an I-owe-you of mine for half a stick of spearmint or the last bite of my next store-bought cookie.

(1)

Before statehood, my father, Howard Kantner, attended the university at College, Alaska. He was seventeen and went to school for various reasons, a degree not being one of them. He liked nature and animals and was a quiet romantic; he dreamed of wild country, anywhere far from Toledo, Ohio. Also, in those days of the draft, Uncle Sam had a number awaiting his name, and a ticket to a wilderness of a more human nature—the Korean War.

He stepped off his first plane ride onto the muddy roads of Fairbanks. A truck drove him to the nearby town of College, cut out of the trees of the Interior. On the University of Alaska campus the streets were gravel, the air was chilly, and the first students he met were no kids; they were men: combat-hardened soldiers, Korean War vets.

"I thought, 'What have I done?'" Howie says. "But Alaska grew on me each day."

Within a short time he had a dog team. He bought a pair of Army surplus snowshoes. He fed his dogs on university commons' scraps. Summers, he roamed Alaska Territory working seasonal jobs as far south as Petersburg: commercial fishing, fighting fire in the Interior, and working as a stream guard in Bristol Bay, keeping commercial fishermen from sneaking inside the river mouth to set their nets. Winters, he attended classes; he trapped furs in the woods and learned from miners and old sourdoughs how to take care of hides, build cabins, stay warm.

In the spring of 1961 he went north; he worked at and around Cape Thompson on the Chukchi Sea coast assisting biologist Peter Lent, his good friend. By then Howie had earned a zoology degree, though he never filled out the final paperwork nor bothered to pick up the certificate. He was in his midtwenties.

His job at Cape Thompson was to gather information on the Western Arctic Caribou Herd. He was in good shape and able to run for miles on the tundra, collecting data on equally fleet-footed newborn calves, taking parasite samples and body measurements. He and Peter were also mapping the range and conducting the first census of the herd, which was estimated to be between 160,000 and 200,000 animals.

It was known that caribou ate lichens during winter months—lichens that absorbed radioactive material from the atmosphere. This radioactivity was concentrated in caribou, and further concentrated in humans who ate the caribou. Additional research was prompted by "Project Chariot," the Atomic Energy Commission's plan to play with its new toys.

Project Chariot intended to use four or five nuclear bombs to vaporize a deep-water harbor at Cape Thompson for future mineral extraction and for Native use. It would be a sort of science-fiction instaharbor, a mile long and deep enough for oceangoing ships, with nice warm glow-in-the-dark shores. The fact that Natives lived off that unpolluted land and ocean, and used *umiat*—skin boats with a draft of less than two feet—did not concern our government. Alaska, for its part, had entered the Union two years before, and the brand-new forty-ninth state was already addicted to military spending and relished any extra attention in that department.

(Recently, I discovered that Edward Teller, the man who helped build the first hydrogen bomb and was the "mastermind" behind Project Chariot, did not immediately disappear in these intervening decades. In addition to conceiving Project Chariot, Teller attempted to talk our government into using a nuclear weapon to blast a hole in the surface of the moon, to search for water needed to colonize it. In more recent times Teller was the father of the fantastically expensive and useless Star Wars missile-defense system. Even as late as the 1990s, and probably up until his death in 2003, this man took part in an effort to persuade the United States to shoot rocketloads of sulfuric ash into the upper atmosphere to reflect sunlight, to practice playing with our climate.)

Near the end of that summer half a century ago along the Chukchi coast, while Howie was doing his job studying caribou, he met an Iñupiaq couple living alone in a sod igloo, eight miles south of the proposed blast site. These were the only Eskimos living between Kivalina to the south and Point Hope to the north. People from Kivalina and Point Hope hunted and gathered in this area, and in the past more families

Mabel and Austin Thomas in front of their buried sod igloo at Cape Thompson, 1962 (Photo by Howard Kantner)

had lived Out. At that time, however, these were the only Native inhabitants along that nearly one-hundred-mile stretch of coastline. The man had one leg. The woman had a bad knee but did the hunting. Their names were Mabel and Austin Thomas.

Mabel spoke few English words; Austin could converse in the language. They wore fur and skin clothing, and they gathered food from the ocean and surrounding tundra. When fall came Howie didn't take the flight back to Fairbanks; he stayed with Mabel and Austin. Peter Lent arranged for the biology project to deliver Howie's four dogs from Fairbanks to Kotzebue, and Nelson Walker, a Kotzebue bush pilot and polar bear hunting guide, flew the small team on north to Cape Thompson.

Mabel taught my father Eskimo ways to hunt and take care of skins. He slept on caribou hides on the floor of the igloo and hunted every day for food for the three of them and their many dogs. Seals, caribou, foxes, ptarmigan, owls—whatever moved, they hunted. He wore sealskin pants, caribou parkas, mukluks, bone sunglasses. Breakfast, lunch, and dinner were variations of raw fish, boiled caribou, white fox, seal meat and oil, berries, and other foods they collected.

Years later, living in our own family sod igloo, when he related these events, enthusiasm rang in his stories: of trying to kill rabid white foxes on a stormy night; of fur-clad travelers arriving, staying, eating the family out of house and home and then traveling on; of drinking seal oil for energy and warmth; of watching hundreds of seals passing one day and not seeing another until the ocean froze; of not washing his hair for the whole winter and how silky it became. His words always went back to Mabel Thomas. He spoke of her always with respect and awe.

"She was like a medicine woman," he still says humbly. "Her dad was an *aŋatkuq,* a shaman. He taught her to hunt with her brothers."

Now, in the twenty-first century, by telephone via various satellites, I dial my parents on their farm in Hawaii, to ask why—why were the Thomases living there alone in 1961 on that storm-swept coast?

At the other end of the line my dad pauses, attempting to find facts in his jumbled memory. And then the answer comes, as ironic as so many of our lives truly are. "They were there because Mabel was cold!"

He sounds as surprised as I am, and talks more, spilling pieces of the past I've never heard. A shelter cabin . . . the mouth of Ogotoruk Stream . . . the bomb site. . . . "Mabel was cold. Oh!—And Austin liked good drinking water."

In Kivalina, flat, low, treeless, and forty miles south along the coast, drinking water came from the river, and wood was hard to come by. Villagers had to travel miles just to cut small willows to burn for heat. Cape Thompson had driftwood—a good place to overwinter—and good ice for drinking. "I remember hauling ice," Howie says, "and sitting on a big log, tired. I was really anemic from deficiencies, from eating all that meat. But I always got my energy back. There were lots of chores to do after hunting. Just like up home at the igloo."

On a second phone, my mom, realistic as always in the face of his innocent romanticism, interjects: "The amazing thing is that Howie didn't get drafted. He was just living on the coast with the Eskimos! And he got deferred. Everybody else was getting drafted." Howie murmurs, "I *wrote* to the draft board in Toledo, told them what I was doing."

I mention what I recently learned about Edward Teller. They utter quick surprise, and Howie jokes, "He was still mad because he didn't get to blow up those bird cliffs."

In the spring of 1962 my father left the Arctic to climb Mount McKinley with a group of friends. Although he was back in the "white world," he had been changed, I think, by that intense life at Cape Thompson. Around Alaska he had gleaned knowledge from gold miners and vets, trappers and commercial fisherman, but it was along the Chukchi coast where his respect for old Iñupiaq ways was born. The tundra and open spaces, the awe-inspiring storms and animals, igloo-dwelling and living close to the land: it had gotten under his skin.

Climbing the mountain, the group chose not the popular path—which starts with a ski-plane flight to Kahiltna Glacier at 7,000 feet—but decided on the Sourdough Route, a trail blazed by four Alaskans in a 1910 attempt to be first to summit McKinley. Those four men had climbing experience similar to my dad's (virtually none) and spent three months to get two of them and a spruce pole to the North Summit. Sadly, not everyone believed them; also, the South Summit happens to be 850 feet higher. Three years later Archdeacon Hudson Stuck took credit for the first "true" ascent of McKinley.

"I didn't care if we made it to the top," Howie says. "That type of thing didn't interest me."

He and his friends' ascent started beside the railroad tracks at park headquarters in Mount McKinley National Park. The five men and one woman—Anore Bucknell, the second woman to summit McKinley—strapped on their heavy wooden skis. The mountain was still a hundred miles in the distance. They skied to the base of it with packs weighing sixty to a hundred pounds and returned to ferry additional loads of gear. "I wasn't interested in the summit," Howie repeats. "I liked skiing and carrying those heavy packs. And being out with that group. They were great. Great people."

The climb took forty-five days, longshoring loads in, working their way up the Muldrow Glacier, climbing from McGonagol Pass on up Karsten's Ridge to Harper's Glacier, following it up to Denali Pass, and summiting. Their party was the first in years to make it up the Muldrow Glacier after it had surged, leaving rugged ice that had turned back previous groups.

By the end of May they were off the mountain. Quickly, they scattered their separate ways, seeking summer work and pursuing responsibilities that had been put on hold. A month later Howie was back in the northwest Arctic.

While the group of friends was on McKinley, a small plane circled them. The passenger door opened, and out sailed a box. The package cometed into the snow. A case of oranges! The person waving, the

The climbers rest along the trip to base camp: Howard Kantner, Keith Jones, Garry Kenwood, Paul Dix (Anore Bucknell and Jim Mack are not in photo), 1962 (Photo by Jim Mack)

one who had pushed the box out, was Erna Strausbourger, a friend
to all of the climbers and a twenty-three-year-old graduate of the
University of Alaska-Fairbanks, then working on a master's degree in
mathematics.

Erna had come north with none of this in mind. She had grown
up in Cleveland and attended Ohio State for two years as a math major. "I was sick of it," she says now. "The school had 20,000 students,
too many people for me. It was like a factory." Erna dropped out and
was living at home and working. Still pressured by her mother to get a
degree, she was casting about for schools as far away as Scotland. The
University of Alaska sent her a nice brochure. They wanted females,
of which the state had a shortage, especially upperclassmen. They also
had a good biology program and promised to transfer all her credits.
In Fairbanks it took her a mere year and a half to graduate. Her aunt
flew north for the graduation. Erna didn't pause, but entered graduate
school and accepted a job as a teaching assistant in biology and anat-
omy. "All of my students were my friends," she says.

Her parents were pleased that things were going well; they expected
their daughter home in a year or two. Then she started traipsing around
with the wrong crowd, doing things like dropping fruit from tiny ski
planes, and dropping out of the master's program. She was a good Jewish girl, smart and pretty, and it seemed the very next thing they knew
she'd married some guy they had never laid eyes on, a man who ran
after caribou and climbed mountains—married him in a windswept
Arctic town called Kotzebue. In a tar paper shack owned by an Eskimo
lady named Mamie Beaver. Holding a bouquet of wildflowers that grew
nearby. Married a Catholic, no less.

Things got worse. In the fall she hitchhiked from Fairbanks to the
East Coast with Howie, and then traveled to Europe with him. They
spent the winter there while he sketched and decided if he wanted to
pursue being an expatriate artist, as opposed to being a white Eskimo.
Neither set of parents was impressed. They'd lived through the Great
Depression; what was wrong with these kids, not settling into careers?

In Alicante, Spain, in December they had a baby. By then, 1963, America was involved in another war. Having a child moved Howie's classification to 2A; he was ineligible to be drafted, ineligible to be sent to Vietnam. The child was healthy, a blond, blue-eyed boy, happy in disposition, and his Gerber baby looks helped relations when the small family returned to Ohio. Helped, that is, until they stuffed their sleeping bags and repacked their Kelty packs, heading north again. "To the ice-box," as Erna's mother said cynically.

Back in Fairbanks, they met up with their friends, including Keith Jones and Anore Bucknell, veterans of the McKinley climb. Keith and Anore —possibly because of continuous conversation with my dad in the days directly after he left Mabel and Austin's igloo, and also because of their own travels in northwest Alaska—had wintered the previous year on the Kobuk River, above the Arctic Circle and a hundred miles inland from the coast. Accompanying them was another Ohioan, Don Williams. They built a sod igloo on the north side of the river. In Spain, my parents had received a letter from Keith and Anore and Don de-scribing a beautiful, wild, and rich area. Onion Portage was the name of the place.

The Arctic had already infiltrated my dad's blood, but the letter and promise of close friends for companions must have helped convince my mom to go north. As a result, in September 1964 a motley group gath-ered at Phillips Field in Fairbanks: my parents and their nine-month-old son, Kole; Keith and Anore Jones, now married; and two single men, Don Williams and Ole Wik. Beside them was a heap of gear and guns and sled dogs.

The Twin Beech airplane that they chartered was supposed to drop them in the tiny new village of Ambler, but the only airstrip there was river ice and the river hadn't yet frozen. The pilot booted them out on a strip near Kobuk village, ninety river miles upstream. There they waited days along the bank until finally they met a man from Ambler, an Iñu-piaq entrepreneur named Tommy Douglas who had a small plank barge that he had made of hand-cut spruce and powered with a diesel engine. Tommy ferried the white people and their dogs down to Ambler.

No one that I recall ever mentioned payment, but there must have been some trade, and Tommy was a friend from then on. My dad adopted Tommy's wife, Elsie, as his *paatnaq*, his partner, and gave her wolverine skins and other furs, and in the early years we stayed with them in their plank house when we traveled to Ambler.

Tommy, like Mabel's husband, Austin, had only one leg. Actually, Tommy did have two legs; it's just that one was made of wood. He didn't let this inhibit his abilities, and in all seasons and all weather he traveled out on a rough land. Alone he had survived a plane crash at the top of Nakmaktuak Pass and the ensuing fire that took his leg.

Here in this history I'm stymied by lack of details, lack of memory, frustrated by vague and contradictory bits of other people's stories; I wasn't even born until February that winter. I would say that here again in this history—as in the case of Project Chariot—everyday events on the frontier, daily chores such as hauling drinking water and finding food, bumped against events on the national stage. Like needle ice shifting and tinkling and being shoved ashore by massive icebergs, the course of lives was changed by these events, lives ultimately connected to that of a scrawny white boy: me. Maybe there is a lesson there, in the power of our small actions, or the ripples caused by large ones.

Onion Portage was where my family and their friends were headed, but it was not where they ended up.

Now, in the information age, Onion Portage is somewhat famous, though thousands of years ago it probably was much more so. The actual portage is directly below a birch and spruce ridge overlooking the river, similar to the bluff I was born and raised on, carpeted with berries in the fall, good walking and good hunting, accessible to both timber and tundra. Onion Portage, though, unlike here, is sheltered from the north wind, sheltered by mountains with jade lying at their base, miles closer to the village, and a magnet for people. It is the land's age-old natural crossing for the Western Arctic Caribou Herd on its fall migration south.

With survival as their barometer, the ancient Iñupiat—themselves new to this continent—had not missed discovering this important natural funnel for fresh meat. Nine thousand years later, Keith Jones also favored the spot.

Keith had been a cowboy in Wyoming when the Army drafted him and shipped him to Fairbanks to be a dentist's assistant. He hated the Army but liked Alaska and wrote to his friend Don Williams about this place, even better than Wyoming. By then Don had been drafted, too, and sent to Germany. Keith must have been a persuasive writer; Don came north after he was discharged, and only a year later Keith talked him further north, to the Kobuk.

Unfortunately for this tight-knit group that included my parents, they were not the only ones interested in Onion Portage. The area had again been discovered, this time in 1941, by a wild, tough graduate student on a log raft. By the 1960s he had become the renowned archaeologist Dr. Louis Giddings, who showed Onion Portage to be the most important archaeological site ever found in the Arctic.

Tommy Douglas in Ambler, 1966 (Photo by Don Williams)

By the summer of 1963, Giddings had nearly finished his extensive work on the coastal beach ridges at Cape Krusenstern. He turned his efforts to Onion Portage. He spent the season there, mapping the area and beginning to dig down toward the bottom of human history in that place, down by the riverbank. Before Freezeup that year he returned to Brown University in Rhode Island, where he spent the winter continuing his tireless efforts, with a little fretting on the side about why he'd steered these back-to-the-landers, Keith and Anore and Don, to choose to construct their sod house in one of the old igloo pits on the ridge directly overlooking his site.

Previous pages:
A bull moose
crossing the river
at Onion Portage

Don Williams had already left for work in Katmai National Park in the spring when Giddings arrived with new information from core samples he'd been studying. "I was afraid you'd build in that one," Giddings told Keith. They had built in a pit that had appeared to have been used by Eskimos just a few hundred years previously. But under those remains Giddings now had found signs of thousands of years of use.

"Well, we picked it for the same reason the old-timers did," Keith says now. "It had a good view. You could look for caribou. It was high enough not to flood at Breakup."

The archaeologist nervously assisted in getting the Joneses to Ambler and Out, to Fairbanks where they got work for the summer. He then promptly had their sod home dismantled and their belongings hauled away. He wasn't happy about anyone messing up the area. And the melted-out crap left by their dog team ended up right where he would enlarge his dig. For his own home, Giddings had claimed a five-acre site at Onion Portage and hired Nelson Greist and his family to build him a log cabin there.

I never met Giddings. He was in a car accident during the winter of 1964 and died of a heart attack caused by his injuries. I only saw in summers the huge pits he left behind. My childhood point of view was that this bossy Outsider had dug up the ground, taken the Natives' arrowheads and ancient stone tools, and then, as white people had a habit of doing, disappeared south—in his case leaving behind a large zone of eroding mud, something my parents and their friends never would have done. As the years unwind I see more, see that he died still working down through the eighteen feet and thirty cultural layers of the site, and that his work wasn't simply finding arrowheads, but preserving and interpreting these irreplaceable clues to Eskimo history.

I have that archaeologist to acknowledge for a couple of things in addition to his contribution to his field: because of him I was born and raised in wind, miles further from people. Also because of him, we did not live at what later was to became a crossing not just for the ancient herds but also for the National Park Service float planes, Alaska Department of Fish and Game caribou-collaring crews in speedboats, Discovery

Channel and Disney visits, hunters, gunfire, Japanese tourists, clicking cameras—all coming together there in Septembers where a river of caribou crosses a river of water. As the years go by I see that here, further downstream, this isolation that grew to be my norm shaped my life.

So, Tommy Douglas's *Bucky Bee* chugged downriver to Ambler. There Don Williams borrowed a large homemade boat, nicknamed the Arc, from Oliver Cameron, a self-styled missionary living in the new village. Don borrowed an outboard motor from Jacob Johnson, an Iñupiaq man, and took the group further downriver, past Onion Portage, where they now had been forbidden to settle. Keith, always with sharp eyes for a good camping spot, knew where he wanted to go next: to a ridge that he'd discovered the spring before, with bare ground and a view.

The newcomers unloaded their possessions in the willows along the shore at the lower end of Paungaqtaugruk. There Don and Ole Wik, both single men, looked upriver and down, across the open tundra. No single women in sight. They foresaw a long winter. They decided they wanted to be nearer to a community and returned upriver with the boat; both built igloos a few miles below Ambler.

A crew excavating the archaeological site at Onion Portage (Roger Hirshland, back left; Shield Downey, front left; Tommy Lee, facing camera; Wilson Tickett, behind Tommy; Willie Goodwin Sr., kneeling; Nelson Griest Sr., standing), 1965 (Photo by Don Williams)

My parents and the Joneses pitched a wall tent. It was mid-September; days were getting shorter, and cold. On a nearby knoll overlooking the tundra they heated rocks to warm the permafrost and dug down to make a house pit, then cut logs and poles and sod and built a small sod igloo. In a time of Eskimos wanting to be like white people, these white people admired the old-life ways.

Local Iñupiaq Harriet Blair, Tommy's daughter, tells me now in horror, "Your parents, they lived like Eskimos!" She shudders. "We wouldn't live like *that*." People still say it, often.

By then my parents and their friends had four or five dogs—a small team that eventually grew to ten or twelve dogs, two small teams— and whipsaws, a keg of gunpowder, and a small pile of iron and brass and glass belongings. They had a stove that was heavy and poor and accepted only kindling. North wind howled almost constantly in the location they chose, this being the reason Keith had found bare ground there the previous spring. If they had asked, local Eskimos would have warned them of this wind, but, alas, communication between cultures is no easy thing. Most likely they did ask but misunderstood the reply.

The first few years the igloo didn't have a door, only a tunnel facing west, with skins over it. The wind roared, burying their home at night; in the morning just a stovepipe protruded out of the snow. In December my brother was one year old. I was born there the first winter, in February 1965. A photograph of Erna in a skin parka on the runners of a dogsled shows a young and pretty woman, though *tough* must have been even truer. Tough to handle the isolation combined with a second pregnancy—and giving birth in what was virtually a cave—the relentless wind, the cold and lack of basic services, and, maybe harder still, turning her back on her education and the dreams attached to it.

(2)

My memory started under snow, there in a dim and freezing-on-the-floor subterranean home, and it coalesced around poorly lit, scary, and exotic events. From the beginning my view of the Arctic and of the

Erna and Howard
in the sod igloo
at Kapikaġvik,
1967 (Photo by
Don Williams)

world in general was, I think, inside out, very different from that of my
parents or their friends or other passers-through. In the wilderness, or
what passed for it, *people* were the exotic creature. The dogs barking
or the drone of an engine brought us boiling outside to scan the sky
and river ice. A dog team in the distance carried a thrill of excitement.
Snowstorms and deep cold, on the other hand, were normal, though
they were events to be respected. In between were animals, from terrifying to tasty, pillars of memory and the spaces in between.

Caribou were most important. Caribou migrated through, alone,
in small groups, or seasonally like benevolent armies marching past.
They provided food, fat, mattress hides, mukluk leggings, parka skins,
sinew for thread, and dog food. They never attacked as bears might,
nor tangled with the dogs like the moose; they didn't chew your
clothes like squirrels did or steal beans the way mice would. Caribou
also brought people.

Most of the "travelers" passing through were Iñupiaq hunters.
Among them, our main visitor was Clarence Wood, a man with nearly

Erna and Kole at
the tunnel entrance
to their sod home,
1965 (Photo by
Howard Kantner)

constant frostbite and good humor. He often spent the night, or sometimes most of the fall, always roaming the land, relentlessly hunting.
His face was frost-scarred in winter, burned dark by sun in spring and
summer. If we heard a motor, Kole's and my first guess was, "Clarence?"
Usually we were correct. He arrived in all weather conditions, in all conditions himself. More than a few times he walked in, his machine broken
down somewhere on the tundra. Once he came with his foot half-frozen
and his snowgo out there sunk; another time he arrived with a big rock
with blue paint on it, feeling high and happy, with a broken collarbone.
He'd rammed the rock in the dark with his Polaris, flown a long way,
knocked himself out on the ice, scared his wife and other passenger—and,
being Clarence, continued on, happy about the adventure of it.

Sometimes he arrived with a bear, or wolf skins, or sled-loads of
geese; countless times he was short of gas or parts, or his sled had broken. Often he just wanted company and coffee. When the ice was melting and it seemed too soft to snowgo or the ice was freezing and it was
too dangerous to be boating, Clarence appeared, rifle across his back,
joking, laughing, shrugging stoically at the tough conditions. "Com'on
now!" he'd retort if we asked how he managed to travel in or on such
bad ice.

In winters when caribou stayed on the tundra across the river from
our house there were more hunters than usual. Other seasons or concentrations of caribou and wolves and wolverines brought travelers
from both upriver and down, people everyone knew: Merrill Morena,
who had grown up along this section of river; Tommy Lee, Charlie
Douglas, Alex Sheldon, Charlie Jones, Nelson Greist, Isaac Douglas,
Shield Downey, and others from Ambler; and Lorrie Schuerch, Lee
Barr, Raymond Stoney, Rudy Black, Clyde Baldwin, and more from
downriver. The downriver hunters were less familiar. They came further,
the trail was deeper, and it was a direction we rarely traveled. Because
they came from Kiana, a bigger and richer village, they had better grub
boxes: Fig Newtons, hot dogs, Butterfingers, real Banquet chicken—
cooked, breaded, and in a box.

Seth and Alvin melting snow on an outdoor woodstove; Alvin's sister Cindy in the background, 1974 (Photo by Erna Kantner)

Hunters often stayed until they got the meat they were hunting, or until they fixed broken parts or help arrived. Kole and I scampered around peering at their unfamiliar belongings. Out in the cold my dad helped them make repairs and eyed their basket sleds for good features. Often the men switched to Iñupiaq and spoke among themselves at our table. Howie liked that; it reminded him of Mabel and her son Willard Adams, and of Oran Knox and his other Kivalina friends. The visitors appreciated the fact that my mom served dried fish and meat and seal oil— *niqipiaq*, Eskimo food. My mom, though, was not always overjoyed with the way these hunters set up camp in our living room, our only room.

Kantner family at Tommy and Elsie's house in Ambler, 1969 (Photo by Tommy Douglas)

Occasionally men came drunk and wanted my dad to join them—which he never once did—or they needed gas, or just stopped to leave something that they had shot and didn't want to haul home, like a loon or a skinny caribou.

One winter Shield Downey spent weeks at our table. Shield had watery eyes and a huge protruding abdominal hernia; years before he had cut his stomach in an accident with a knife. Days, he'd snowgo out to shoot caribou and cut the legs off and return to stack the animals in our yard; nights, he'd relentlessly beat my brother and me at checkers, never allowing us to win. When a north wind in March buried all his caribou he "broke camp" and went back upriver. After Breakup, one after another, the brown backs of the animals melted out.

On our table there was always food from the land, mostly meat of one kind or another. Caribou, moose, black and brown bear, beaver, muskrat, lynx, fox, squirrel, porcupine, grouse, rabbit, ptarmigan, more

Seth wrapped in a hide to stay warm while his parents take care of fresh caribou, 1967 (Photo by Erna Kantner)

caribou—caribou pot roast, tongue, tenderloins, lips and leg bones, rendered back and intestine fat—and crane, swan, goose, ground squirrel, seal oil, whale blubber, loon, duck, otter. We ate eyes and hearts and paws, then scraped and tanned the skins with sourdough and alder bark. We and the dogs ate fish, too. Cooked fish, raw fish, dried fish, frozen raw fish, frozen raw stink-fish, fish eggs, fish heads, boiled fish intestines. Salmon, trout, sharpnose whitefish, roundnose whitefish, suckers, pike, sheefish, mudshark, grayling. In the spring we ate fireweed shoots, bluebell shoots, lousewort, willow leaves, wild onions, pussy willows, birch sap, cottongrass stems. In the summer, wild rhubarb, mushrooms, sourdock. In the fall we picked cranberries, blueberries, highbush cranberries, salmonberries, crowberries, rose hips, tinniq berries, stinkweed. My parents asked elders and travelers alike how to live the old ways. Always, they were asking, listening, collecting food, collecting wood, collecting wisdom.

My brother and I, well . . . we weren't exactly like our parents. Times were changing in the Arctic. When we were small boys and my family traveled to the village a couple times each winter—and later to fish camp on the coast across the water from Kotzebue—we ran into low stone walls of racism that my parents never saw. Every breath we drew in these places came with the reminder that we were white, different, and therefore at least partially wrong. We fell back on things that made sense. More and more, Kole studied books with equations and laws that couldn't be bent: physics, mathematics, electrical theory. I also turned to something unequivocally impartial, though in the complete opposite direction: the land.

We both saw our bush life of dogs and animals and seasons as unremarkable. We explored the tundra and riverbanks and went barefoot until the snow got too deep; we swam in the ice floes for waterfowl we had wounded; we blew up ptarmigan crops and bear bladders for balloons, gnawed the layer under the bark on new shoots of willow and birch twigs, chewed spruce pitch into gum, gathered tern eggs, ate duck feet. We sucked the sweet pollen off mosquitoes' faces and spat them back out alive. And always we kept sharp eyes up the river and down for any human young.

One of those, Alvin Williams, half Eskimo and two and a half years old, hit me over the head with an empty one-gallon can when I was

Keith and Anore building a second sod igloo near the first one built with the Kantners, 1966 (Photo by Don Williams)

four. I ran for my grubby green pillow. The bonk caused blood and possibly other deficiencies. Alvin and I grew up as best friends—who saw each other only half a dozen times a year—hunting and running dogs together and assuming that was the life we would lead, he with his family in the village and me with mine way down the river. By then Don Williams had married Nelson Greist's daughter, Mary, and they settled half a mile west of Ambler. Their house, to me, was the far end of the known world. Beyond it was the uncertainty of the villages and fish camps where a white and untested kid's frozen face mask likely would be yanked from behind and sawed into his lips. The most common greeting was "Wanna fight?"

At home downriver, young company was rare and memorable, though for a time when I was four, five, and six a brief flurry of people came to settle and try living near where I was born. White people. Strangers to the North.

It would be another three decades before I questioned why these white newcomers had come and what they were looking for—something about forces down in the States, a back-to-nature movement? Surely nothing that made a bit of sense to or concerned kids born into the Arctic. We were more worried about what shot further in a slingshot, a rock or a used .22 bullet, and who could stand barefoot longest on snow.

Hippies, people called these strangers, my parents included, although they didn't smoke dope or drink and mostly had college degrees. Each and all were very different, though, with different outlooks and dreams, some wanting to build empires of a sort and others, like my dad, wanting to leave as little mark as possible. One winter there were nineteen people living nearby: Keith and Anore built directly below our house, Pete and Barbara MacManus two

Seth peeling bark off spruce slabs, 1969 (Photo by Erna Kantner)

miles upriver, Ole and Sasha Wik below them, and Epsteins a quarter mile up the bluff from our place. They all built sod igloos, and the size, shape, and location of those structures reflected their individual personalities. Ole's igloo was in a tight draw, tall and small and nearly invisible from the riverbank a few yards away. Pete MacManus's was furthest upriver, large and multileveled; Epsteins' close against the bluff and out of the wind. Also, at that time, there were three young men here along the river: Jim Dixon with the MacManuses, and Lenny Kamerling and Carl Vandervort staying with Bob and Annie Epstein and their twin boys in their twelve-by-sixteen dwelling.

In the candlelight of memory, I recall Danny, an Epstein twin, and me playing behind the windbreak logs behind our igloo, poking sticks in the moss and thwacking birch trunks. He had just arrived, and he taught me a new word that started with *God* and ended with *mitt*. We were four and a half. My dad came by heading up the hill, dark sweater, calloused hands, hauling something, a broadsaw or a spruce pole, across his shoulder. He stopped, swung it to the side.

"Maybe that's not a good word," he suggested.

"Why?" Danny shot back. "My dad says it."

This was an understatement. I poked my stick in the ground and glanced over to see the reaction. Howie nodded a couple times, considering Danny's logic. My dad had that way about him; acceptance. How people chose to live was not something he cared to judge. This very much included his belief that if people wanted to live off the land they should be allowed to come north and cut logs or poles and build a cabin or an igloo and try life on the land. Maybe this openness of his fit well with the old Eskimos and, conversely, made a prison out of Toledo. It seemed he had traveled to the far end of the settled world before finding what he liked.

During the fall there was a falling out in Epsteins' cramped igloo that involved more new words. When the ice was thick enough to cross the river, Carl crossed and built a last-minute sod-and-pole shelter before winter.

By Breakup the young men were gone. Come summer the Epsteins tried to garden using fish from the river for fertilizer. Bears visited themselves upon the scene. Summers were choked with mosquitoes. The overconcentration of nature didn't nurture the couple's marriage. Soon they were gone, separate ways.

MacManuses, after their second winter, moved upriver to the village. Anore's younger brother, Don Bucknell, visiting the valley for the first time and, being helpful, attempted to warm the Jones's igloo for them, this without realizing that even a snow-covered sod roof will burn. Clarence Wood appeared off the tundra just in time to spot the first flames. The fire was spectacular in the north wind, fueled by boxes of books and journals and exploding ammunition. At that point Keith and Anore, too, moved upriver and rebuilt half a mile above Ambler. A group of non-natives including Don Bucknell and Bob Schiro were settling there near Dan and Joyce Denslow, the village's first schoolteachers. The Wiks soon followed suit. These people and others stayed on in Ambler, although they often camped near my family during Breakup and Freezeup. Regardless, in the span of a year or two we were alone, miles and miles across country from the nearest neighbors, the village.

I'm not certain what uncertainty does for kids. There was always meat but questions too: What would happen if our dad fell through the ice, or if our mom got sick? If the wind opened our skylight, or a moose walked down the ridge and fell through the roof? What if the Bureau of Land Management burned our house as they threatened to do because my parents had chosen not to claim the land? What if a bear came in our new caribou-skin door? It was no secret that our parents had left their world for this isolated, semi-Eskimo existence, yet the wave of other people seemed to be drawn back to the lands of humans. I don't know why we didn't follow, but it never seemed to be a question. My dad felt most comfortable out on the edge, away from people. He loved this country and this life, and he worked hard, always, to avoid the one thing he did not want—a job.

Kole and Seth waiting with the dogs, 1967 (Photo by Erna Kantner)

When Bob Epstein still lived here, he and Pete MacManus were friends. Around the time that they ordered a roll of trapping wire together they had had disagreements, and one or the other wasn't happy with the split or who got the spool, and they weren't friends after that. Bob had a chain saw and he felled trees on the bluff and milled boards for the walls of his igloo. Inside the structure he chain-sawed a giant chair out of a stump. The chair was straight-backed, too-tall, hard, and uncomfortable. He covered it with caribou hide, fur up.

Caribou hair is hollow, for warmth, and because of that it is brittle. Most of us slept on caribou hides and wore caribou socks and mukluks, and a few of us wore caribou parkas. All of us and our stuff at all times were sprinkled in caribou hair. This included strays in the soup and tea. Bob's chair was worse, a great clinging furry mess.

35

These back-to-the-land newcomers were that way; they tried new things. You were not likely to see a Native with a caribou hair chair shedding all over his living room. These newcomers, though, were fairly well received in the region. Often they didn't know what they were doing and locals saw them less as a threat than as strange large white children, comical in their mistakes and in the outlandish gear they tried.

Later, after the Epsteins had gone and weren't coming back, Pete boated down in his plank boat, the old Arc, which he'd bought from Oliver Cameron. He salvaged the Epstein place for abandoned supplies and boards to use to add on to his sod igloo in Ambler. After Pete's salvage efforts, the house became sod mounds marking the perimeter of hewn floorboards, fallen shelves, and corner posts. Runoff, which during their first spring had been a nasty surprise sluicing through Bob and Annie's living room, now cascaded down the bluff, eroding the ruin. Rapidly the place faded back into the earth. Kole and I helped; barefoot and leery of rose thorns and nails, we rooted around in the damp depression. In the middle was the sodden hairy heap of Bob's old chair. We scraped crud and squirrel cones and mushrooms aside. We found treasures: bulged and blackened cans of fruit cocktail, big boxes of non-dairy creamer, even a dark gray spool—trapping wire!

We hauled the stash down the bank to the rocks and along the shore home. My mom met us at the door with her dietary beliefs: refined sugar was the devil, chemicals were lieutenant demons, and we weren't allowed to eat that non-dairy creamer stirred up with warm water in a mug. Our utilitarian lifestyle, though, didn't condone throwing anything away, not without waiting awhile in case a use was found. Maybe it would make good bait, or glue. The non-dairy creamer went into a corner of our food cache. Our dad thanked us for the trapping wire, and it went under the workbench.

About that time Kole and I first trapped professionally, as bounty hunters. My parents offered seven cents for a shrew, five cents for a vole, what everyone called a mouse.

In the back of the igloo between where the floorboards ended and the poles of the wall leaned, Kole knelt down and started digging a hole in the dirt. He used one of our toys, a jade ax that Keith or Howie had found somewhere. It was chipped and beaten; we boys had spent time with hammers, trying to break off pieces of jade. Kole had bitten finger-nails and big triangle feet, like a black bear's. He buried a three-pound Maxwell House coffee can to the rim and tamped it in precisely. Above it he hung a piece of raw caribou meat on a string. Over the can he put a sheet of paper with an X knifed in the middle and dirt sprinkled around the edges. Probably if I hadn't hogged the few store-bought Victor mousetraps we owned he never would have designed that trap. The Victors were no bargain, though, grimed gray with moldy blood and mouse drool, gnawed, with loose staples, and touchy-triggered.

The next day was tough, a bad day in the annals of little-broth-erhood. Maybe a mouse or two got into my traps. Possibly I made a dime. Kole knelt beside the corner post, his yellow-handled needle-nose pliers in his hand. He needed the pliers to retrieve tails among the scrapes of fur and feet, to cash in to claim his bounty. Shrews and mice had dropped into the can all night and had eaten each other.

The following night he didn't catch quite as many. But I caught none. No shrew was going to mess around an old trap when he could go next door to the cannibal party.

Eventually Kole went back to his experiments with batteries and wire and magnets he'd pounded out of broken radios from the Ambler dump. More than trapping, he liked to read and to experiment with the electron-ics kit that old college friends of my parents, Bruce and Joan Foote, had sent from Fairbanks. He read every book on our shelves. When our cor-respondence school sent a complete set of World Book encyclopedias, he read them all, starting on the snowdrift out in front of Don and Mary's house half an hour after we left the village post office with the box.

As for me, the year after the mouse-trapping disaster I begged for dogs, made a sled out of birch, trapped three foxes. Made sixty-eight dollars, eighty-six dollars, and ninety dollars respectively from Seattle

Fur Exchange. The first fox I skinned I cut eighteen holes in the hide. The second, six. The third, a pretty red female, only three. That didn't count the holes I cut in my hands. Our dad had a feel for animals and was a talented trapper. He taught us how to track weasels and later foxes and bigger animals, and how to skin and dry the furs. Lee Barr, from Kiana, started calling me "Trapper" when he passed through. I was going to be a trapper. And a hunter. And maybe play guitar like Don and Ole and Woody Guthrie.

Six years before that, before Ole and Sasha moved to Ambler, it happened that our family had dog-teamed to their igloo a mile and a half upriver, to visit or maybe hear them sing and play guitar, or maybe to borrow flour or powdered milk—who remembers? Howie ran behind the sled runners as he always did; my mother rode in the basket with us two kids wrapped in caribou skins and in our fur parkas with caribou skin mittens, thumbless and sewn on for simplicity and safety. It was December. On the ice in front of Wiks' igloo, a huge brown bear appeared. Bears were supposed to be asleep in their dens. To see a bear in midwinter was as disconcerting as seeing a camel, or a game warden.

The adults had time to watch it scent the dogs, then the bear charged. Ole's gun was iced up. He sloshed boiling water down the barrel and on the bolt. The firing pin remained frozen. My dad shot. The dogs barked, excited and scared. Brown fur blurred in the rifle scope, bounding toward him. He fired again, and again, knowing that his wife and kids were nearby.

The bear, once it fell and was skinned and gutted, proved to have worn and broken teeth. It was big and old and so skinny that we didn't eat it, a fact that forever seemed sacrilegious. The dogs ate it, and the hide made us a nice couch.

That couch became central in my first memories. It was brown and furry, warm and comforting and yet made from something fearful. When we climbed up on it our feet were off the cold floor and away from mice scurrying around. Before bedtime, my mom read to us on the couch. She had been a whiz at college, with fine clothes (not furs, apparently) and a sharp memory. She stressed proper grammar, not what travelers spoke and I hoped to learn. Those stories she read aloud went into my head and got cached alongside stories brought by respected hunters such as Clarence, Charlie Jones, and others.

Like the gold and finery in fairy tales, Iñupiaq riches were straightforward things, easy to grasp: furs, skins, and fat meat were riches. Above those and bordering on magical were strength and endurance, a good rifle, and a good lead dog, possessions valued for acquiring more meat, furs, and skins. This was true until the arrival of Snow Travelers. Soon they ruled. Dog teams began to disappear. Semiautomatic rifles became the guns of choice.

Our mom was also our schoolteacher, home-schooling us from lesson books sent by Centralized Correspondence Study in Juneau. At his workbench Howie provided distraction: measuring gunpowder, skinning animals, or sawing boards to make sleds. He sawed a lot. Sometimes he pounded, or rasped, and our teacher reprimanded him, telling him to be quieter so we could study. At night when we studied I would glance over from the tedium of textbooks, watching his ripsaw rise and fall, my mind making words out of the rhythmic sound. My mom would attempt to get my attention back; she worked hard to teach spelling, grammar, and phonics. It was hopeless. I wanted to be a hunter; hunters didn't carry those things. In my head daydreams floated in a moat of unsorted facts and fables, and all those verbs and adjectives, monikers and modifiers, sank into a slurry of nonsense. No one spoke of dyslexia; I assumed that old-fashioned stupidity was what kept me writing my numbers backward and unable to learn left from right.

In Ambler, Don Williams owned a guitar and knew how to play it. Regularly, his son Alvin and I pestered him to get the instrument out, usually with no luck. When he did play, we sat on the floor and watched his fingers, listened and smiled. He sang western songs with *hoss*, *ain't* and *them boys*. "Froggy Went a'Courtin'." "The Battle of San Juan Hill." Music, mixed with the glamorous impertinence of bad grammar! Ole and Sasha played instruments and sang, too, but with correct pronunciation.

Unfortunately, company was rare and a rifle, not a guitar, was the first item people leaned on their sleds. Music happened about as often as Christmas. And, like store-bought presents, it remained something that could only be manufactured by other people.

Every winter, the day after Kole's birthday we boys cut a Christmas tree. It didn't matter if a blizzard was blowing—frostbite would heal. We bundled up, grabbed hatchets and the snowshoes Oliver Cameron had made for us, and ran down the snowdrifts to hitch up Bonehead and Murphy and the other dogs to pull the tree home. One of us rode; the other had to pant behind or in front of the dogs. By then the sun was gone for a couple of weeks, leaving only orange beyond the mountains at noon and darkness the rest of the day.

On the way home we were careful not to knock all the needles off the frozen tree. We carried it down snow steps and squeezed it inside our igloo. The needles turned white with frost and that poor tree woke up thirsty. The base went in a one-pound coffee can, and we got out our manila envelope of ornaments. The best were the real plastic glow-in-the-dark ornaments from MacManuses. We strung popcorn and used trapping wire to attach small Hanukkah candles to the limbs. There wasn't much room in the corner. Howie was usually bending runners or making a sled across what floor space there was.

Kole and I scoured the walls and workbench and junk boxes for presents. We slipped out to the caches, climbed the ladders, and rummaged through our parents' supplies, trying to manufacture gifts. Our family traveled to town only a few times between September and May. The first trip usually aligned with the dentist's visit to town. Ambler was far, and days too short in December for my parents to be interested in the travails of the trip. And mixing with people meant catching colds and the flu, and we often returned sick. We didn't have spare money and there wasn't much to buy besides food at Tommy Douglas's and Mark Cleveland's stores. Our mom mail-ordered presents in advance. She put foresight into it and was stealthy. She had been raised Jewish, and our dad raised Catholic, but she was the one who made Christmas. He would have made three or four kinds of cookies, then gone back to sawing boards.

One Christmas Kole received a rectangular ivory-colored box. Inside were bird pictures, used, of course. Familiar sparrows and chickadees, and blue jays we'd never seen. At first Kole thought they were photographs, but the cards turned out to be shockingly perfect paintings. Nature paintings: momentarily interesting, but ultimately disappointing. We had enough nature. It wasn't something we wanted polluting Christmas. And drawings of it were less valuable than the kind that went into the soup pot.

The bird pictures were from Howie and they definitely didn't require batteries. Nor were they plastic glue-together model airplanes like our mother might order. Those were real presents. Over the years we received and built a dozen or so World War II bombers and fighters and battleships, planes and boats that were in some of the novels we read and much more exciting to bush kids than art—the epitome of inedible, useless, and weird.

In February my birthday came along and I received a wrapped rectangular gift from Kole. In March, my dad got the bird pictures back. He had quit drawing by that time. His charcoal pencils, pastels, and paints were scattered in his junk boxes. Eventually, one Christmas even my mom received the ivory-colored box. The corners were getting tattered. Kole and I took it out of Howie's brass bread box to give to her. Through the years, it came to be a family expression. Given a small, flat present, one of us would groan: "Ugh, I hope it's not the Bird Pictures."

Most days were windy, drifting snow—not birthdays, and no travelers coming. It was just the four of us, and the huge horizons. Sometimes it was so cold and silent that ice fog formed over a single moose on the river, and we could hear ptarmigan pecking willows a half-mile off. Days, Kole chipped the ice to open the water hole and hauled buckets of water that froze on the way up the hill. I shoveled out rounds of

Don and Mary (with
Alvin behind her)
leave for Ambler
by dog team, 1969
(Photo by Erna
Kantner)

firewood and carried them inside. More frequent than silence was the north wind. It shook the roof, buried the door, and made high drifts and cornices. Kole and I skied and slid and dug snow tunnels and occasionally built a snow igloo. We sealed the dogs in our caves and let them chase each other through the mazes.

Down below the drifts, beyond the dog yard, was the burn barrel. Fire was fun, but there was seldom much to burn. Paper and cardboard went into the woodstove; food scraps went in the dog pot. We rarely ate canned food, and cans were cut open on both ends, pounded flat, folded, and then burned.

One day after we finished our chores, we were there at the barrel trying to get a fire to catch. Kole noticed something interesting: one of our parents had finally thrown out a box of non-dairy creamer. We opened the sharp little metal pour spout. Inside was a fine white powder. Kole peered in and dumped a little on the smoldering fire. It flashed flame in his face. We jumped back, eyes wide. We took off our mittens and scooped a handful each. It was cold and dusty. We tossed it over the barrel. WHOOOWH! An astonishing mushroom cloud ignited the air.

We shook each other's shoulders and laughed with glee.

Thought and reinforcements were required. We pushed our hands into our mittens and ran up the drifts to the house. Carefully, we chose a fighter airplane and a bomber. Kole got his needle-nose pliers and we heated wire in the stove and burned fake bullet holes along the fuselages. The sojourn was over. These planes and their little plastic pilots were going to war.

Two boys on the edge of the tundra and riverbank, down below the north wind drifts, one boy small and one big, dressed in mismatched patched snowgo suits, caribou socks, mink mittens, ermine fur sewed in around our throats to thaw our chins; the chained sled dogs idly glancing over from their circles of gnawed bones, shit, and yellow pissicles. Maybe we didn't have neighbors, toys with batteries, songs, or seldom a friend, but until the last box of non-dairy creamer was gone, we had nuclear weapons!

43
non-dairy creamer

Following pages: First day of Freezeup; Seth retrieves fish nets and hunts caribou before pulling the boat for winter, 1989 (Photo by Stacey Glaser)

counting fish

In the fall when Bonehead and Murphy and the other dogs still lay in the willows, useless on the ends of their chains and flopped out in the dirt, we worked the river, every day gathering fish for their winter food. The dogs were mine and my brother's from the time we were eight and nine. Our parents had gotten rid of their team a few years earlier. My dad, with the passing years, had lost heart for dog mushing. He'd always had small teams, and two of his best dogs died when Elsie Douglas in Ambler was taking care of them, his leader from eating a tasty Brillo pad Elsie tossed out with the dishwater. He gave away what was left of his team, tired also of the endless seasons of killing stacks of caribou for the hungry dogs. He bought a snowgo, but the machine spent most of its time under a tarp while he gratefully walked, skied, or snowshoed in the silence of the land.

When I was seven I started asking for sled dogs, and my parents acquiesced. They first let me borrow a few from Keith and Anore for a winter. They were unruly dogs, bigger than I was and handy at jumping up and clawing my face. I built a sled, and then another when the birch runners on the first one snapped.

The following summer Kole and I got puppies from Herbert Foster, an Iñupiaq dog musher we camped near at Nuvurak on the coast. Strangely, after getting rid of their own dogs, my parents didn't begrudge the endless catching fish, cutting, stacking, hauling, drying, storing, and worrying about fish for these dogs.

Kole and I trained the pups and sewed collars and harnesses for them. We were partners in feeding and taking care of the dogs and later in trapping with them, but Kole was never a driving force behind having a team. He would have preferred to study, read, or do experiments. He also enjoyed heavy menial labor: chiseling a hole five feet down through the ice for water, or shoveling snow for hours to dig out lost sleds and our buried boat.

The first boat we used for checking our fish nets was an old spruce-plank boat that Oliver Cameron had sold to my family for a hundred dollars. He'd built it with a rise in both stem and stern, and later, buried under the snow, it got bent by snowdrift creep. In the end it was shaped like a banana and was equally tippy. Boats were homemade in those days, mostly long, narrow, low riverboats. They had cotton cloth between the boards and they dried out in the winter. In the spring when folks launched them, water seeped in, and down they sank, riding low to the gunwales. In a day or two the boards swelled up, the river dropped, and people could stroll down with buckets and bail out their boats.

Later, under Oliver's tutelage, my dad built a twenty-four-foot ply-wood fishing boat. It was green and didn't leak for many years. We anchored it along the bank above the dog yard, near the fish racks. When we were teens, and useful as slave labor, Howie started building a boat every spring, to try his hand at a new craft and augment building sleds as a source of cash.

Like any bush chore, we checked our fish nets at that comfortable time somewhere between when we felt like it and when it had to be done. Kole and I ran down the steep path from our door to the shore, and Howie followed behind, careful and eyeing the horizon for movement. Because he was outside most of the day, every day, his eyes uncon-sciously knew where every clump of brush, drift stump, and cutbank was, up and down the river and back on the tundra. If an animal was out there, he spotted it, usually almost instantly, as if some part of his mind already knew it was there.

Howard with a rare king salmon caught in the net, 1976 (Photo by Erna Kantner)

At the bottom of the hill, we passed the fish racks. Gray jays glided to nearby willows. In the grass mice rustled. Kole and I scanned for caribou and for unnoticed porcupines, and then unsnapped the dogs. They sprinted back and forth. The boat motor fired to life, and they swiveled and raced down the shore to swim out to the rock bar. Exercise was important to prepare their muscles for winter work, and they were good, entertaining company, each with his own personality. Murphy led, and listened; Bonehead swam like a drowning person, splashing water over his head.

My dad drove the boat, at half throttle. He didn't allow gas or the motor to be wasted. Driving for pleasure did not happen. We could drive our dog team whenever we felt like it, but that required snow, so we missed winter whenever it was gone.

The best eddy was a quarter mile below the house. The old Eskimos, of course, knew that; the point was named Kapikaġvik, "place where they spear salmon." We set a four-and-a-half-inch mesh whitefish net at the current line of the eddy, and a torn and ratty six-inch mesh net down a dozen yards to weed out the powerful snaggle-toothed salmon working their way up the current. For each net, a spruce pole pounded into the rocks was the shore anchor, a big rock the outer anchor, a Clorox or Wesson oil jug the buoy.

Thankfully, we didn't make fishnet webbing from scratch the way we made most other things—the way Jacob Johnson and other villagers once did, working all winter with twine and knots, hunched at a stump with a nail pounded in. Our webbing was mail-ordered from Memphis

Net and Twine. We dyed it green in a steel bucket, and with net needles hung it to cork line threaded through a mishmash of commercial corks and wooden floats. Along the bottom of the webbing we hung lead weights or lead line.

Late in August the days stayed warm, though they were often rainy. As the season progressed it turned to north wind and bitter cold, or low clouds and snow falling onto the water. The river was wide, clear, and cold, and our fingers went numb and red. Regardless, it was exciting to pull up the cork line and see what rose out of the depths snared in the webbing. In the smaller mesh we caught pike, suckers, grayling, sharpnose and roundnose whitefish, and occasional trout, sheefish, and *tiktaaliq*.

A few days of rain would bring the river up. In the night it might rise, and by morning it moved along faster, brown and muddy, logs coming down and little islands of sudsy foam riding the current. The nets caught few fish and would be full of sticks and twisty black roots.

Back at shore, it was warmer out of the wind. The boat was slippery and hard to stand in, and we moved stiffly in our rain pants. Kole and I picked the still-flopping pike out of the bilge, bonked them, and then hauled the washtubs of fish up the bank and dumped them in the trampled grass. The fish were slimy and bloody, and the female salmon leaked eggs glistening like orange pearls. Kole and I stood across the heap from each other, toeing the fish, contemplating them and the work ahead, and keeping an unconscious ear out for the drone of a motor upriver or down. Complaining about work didn't enter our thoughts, and if it had it would have shamed us. Cutting fish was vaguely fun, or at least satisfying when it was over, but stashed in our minds were memories of music, rare movies, and Dairy Queen, none of which existed along the river.

On the trail our mom was coming toward us, carrying her *ulu* and knives and sharpening stones. We all cut fish—double fillet on one side, backbone on the other—and hung them on spruce poles to dry for people food and dog food. Heads, guts, suckers, and grayling went into the third-of-a-drum dog cooker. Kole snatched grass and broke brush and built a fire under the cooker pot to boil the fish and scraps, to kill the tapeworms before feeding the soup to the dogs.

No-see-ums and whitesocks clouded around our eyes and walked up our sleeves as we worked. The dogs watched us, scratched, played, or dozed on their sides with their ears in the dust. They were bored again now, bug bitten, waiting for winter, half done shedding and skinny. We knew they needed to be fattened up before cold weather came. We glanced up while we worked, for caribou coming through the yard, or at any whine from the dogs, often the first sign of a bear, moose, or other animal passing through. If their noses went up we dropped our slimy knives before they could bark, grabbed a willow, and whipped the ground—and sometimes the dogs—to keep them silent until we determined the direction, distance, animal, and if hunting was to take place. The season decided whether we could preserve the meat, if we needed it, and if the taste was fat and right. Fall was the beginning of a new year, a time of gathering fish and meat and berries for another winter, getting ready for snow.

One day in mid-September, Howie would sniff the air or glance out over the tundra or notice the dying grass and decide it was late enough to start burying fish in the grass to ferment for people and dogs. Mabel Thomas up at Cape Thompson had taught him how to make stink fish. Kole and I never questioned or even really learned his judgment, just followed his directions. We ate that *quaq*—frozen fish—all winter, raw and dipped in seal oil. The dogs got theirs, too, although it was not sliced and minus the seal oil. The *quaq* pile, as we called it, was a welcome relief. No cutting or gutting was required. No building more fish racks, nor loose dogs knocking them over. No bears and birds sliding fish off the poles and vanishing into the grass or the sky. Or worse: misjudging the rain and ending up with all pale and soggy by morning.

We dumped the tubs near the *quaq* pile and made a rough count. A large whitefish was the standard. One large whitefish equaled one. A grayling and a small pike, one. A large sheefish, three or four. Nothing

Caribou crossing
the shallows

was exact, nor drudgery. It was simply what we did, but it had to be
done. And when we were done adding the daily catch, Howie put the
fattest ones aside for people food, then heaped grass and a few spruce
slabs over the pile to keep animals out.

In the evening, after the dog pot had cooled, we fed the dogs. They
gulped the soup down, wagging and rolling their eyes warily, somehow
leaving fine bones and fish eggs in the bottoms of their cut-off five-gallon-can dog bowls.

Before the darkness settled, Howie sent one of us down to the shore
with our school thermometer. We stood, toes sinking into the freezing
mud, holding the thermometer under the water. Waiting, we watched
the current along the shore for the swirl of grayling and listened to great
horned owls across the river hooting in the dusk, and mice tunneling in

the frosty grass. Sometimes caribou silhouetted, splashing in the shallows out to the sandbar. When the water temperature dropped to thirty-four degrees, the next day was net-pulling day. By that date the deck and insides of the boat were iced with eggs and slime, and checking net our fingers turned stiff and we felt lucky to each have at least one insulated rubber glove that didn't leak too badly.

Sometimes a cold night surprised us. In the morning, ice would have frozen out from shore. The boat would be frozen in, with white-edged pans wheeling down the current, bumping the outer edge of the fast ice, tearing huge holes in our nets. Then the exciting first day of winter felt tragic.

After the ice froze thick enough to walk on, our family packed packs and shovels and tools and headed upriver to Paungaqtaugruk. The first trip was arduous, two miles and slow going. Along the way, Howie checked the ice with a *tuuq*, an ice chisel. The dogs whined to go, and they howled mournfully and in unison after we had disappeared up the grassy shore.

Where open water and current cut close to the beach or where the ice was too thin, we scrabbled along cutbanks, climbing the frozen dirt and beating east against dusty west-leaning willows. If fresh snow had fallen, the ice was hard to read. Kole and I stopped often to sweep it aside and lie down, shade our eyes, and peer down through the ice. On the bottom were beautiful pebbles and smooth silt, sunken logs, and sometimes darting fish. In places there was only the dark green blackness of water. Tiny gray bubbles were frozen in the ice. Larger white bubbles marked areas that might break, and silvery bubbles showed how thick the ice had frozen.

Along the shore big brown bear tracks pressed down the thin snow. Howie pointed out the news in the snow: old fox trails and new wolf tracks, moose prints with pointed hooves, caribou with splayed ones, and mink, ermine, and other bouncy, paired tracks. Otters left slide marks, heading out toward the dark water. We carried too much fishing gear to bring along a rifle; we eyed the thickets and the timbered draw where Ole Wik's abandoned sod igloo hunkered in the ground like a bear den.

Offshore was cold blue current, no longer the water of summer but now that of winter, swift and with a vise of cold to seize your chest—treacherous, a lonely liquid death, what people taught their children to fear more than any bear. *Open water!*

At Paungaqtaugruk, a quarter mile above MacManuses' old igloo, the water was slow and deep and partially frozen over. Along the sheer bluffs, whitefish spawned and other fish rested, hunted, and stole each others' eggs. Over the deepest water we chopped a line of spaced holes, parallel with the current and the exact length of each of our nets. Kole lowered a sock filled with rocks down to the bottom while our dad used a long spruce pole with a caribou antler lashed to the end to hook the rope and stretch it under the ice. After he retrieved the sock, we moved to the hole he had used and he strode to the next with the hook. Our hands got cold standing there, and if we let the sock touch the ice it froze down, and then, because the sock was old and had been darned a lot before being retired to net sinker, it would tear and dump its load.

When the rope was stretched under the ice, we used it to pull our first net under. Under-ice nets had small floats, designed to barely float and not raise the net up against the bottom of the ice where it would freeze in. Along the lead line, chunks of antler and old wool socks filled with rocks kept the net on the bottom. At each end we tied a twenty-pound rock and cut a spruce sapling to freeze in and snub off the top line.

The first day was long, with the walk and then hours of sweaty chopping and cold kneeling untangling nets. The air was fresh and icy in our lungs, and at the end of that work waited the trail home in twilight.

The excitement of checking the nets for the first time made the trek upriver faster in the morning. The ice over the fishing holes had frozen a couple of inches thick. Now we chopped open only the holes at each end. At the upstream end, we pulled the heavy rock up and stacked the

net beside it. Roundnose whitefish—fat and big and what we were after—flopped up onto the ice. Tiny pale eggs squirted out of the females and floated away in the current. Grayling swarmed at the mouth of the hole, gulping eggs. We pried the webbing out of their gills and shook the fish free and nudged them aside with our boots. They caked with snow and froze down, their eyes glazing over quickly in the cold.

When the last mesh was checked, one of us jogged to the lower end and pulled the rope we had trailed under the ice, and the net followed it back again into the depths. The stiff frozen webbing made ticking noises, snapping free where it had frozen down, a hard freeze sometimes raising a shout to halt for a second. The net settled back into position. We counted and stacked the fish, and squeezed eggs into a plastic bag. Then we moved to the next net.

After the checking was done, Kole and I got our reward. We unwrapped fishing lures, cut a section of willow and a tiny strip of chin skin off a whitefish, for bait, and jigged for grayling. Later, when a trail was in, old ladies upriver in Ambler would buy them to eat frozen raw. Of course we had to keep the foxes and ravens from stealing them, and had to sled the fish twenty-five miles with our small team. But jigging was enjoyable, and sometimes good wages too—a dollar for only eight fish. Not counting the two-day round-trip journey to deliver them.

At home, my mom wrote on the calendar: eighty-three whitefish, seven suckers, three pike, one salmon. My dad whipped the thawing fish eggs in a bowl. He added cranberries and a little sugar and kept whipping with his hand until the *ittukpalak* was light and pink and fluffy. We pulled stumps and chairs up to the table and ate it by the bowlful, dessert before dinner.

A few days into ice fishing, the trail froze enough to hitch up the dogs and mush upriver along the glare ice, and to haul fish back on the sled. Unlike early fall fish, these fish froze hard and clean and separate, perfect all winter to toss to each dog each night. Ice fishing went on for weeks or a month. We needed roughly two thousand fish to make it

Previous pages: A cold fall morning along the Kobuk.

Fox, bear, and
wolf tracks leading
up a creek.

Kole and Willow
jigging for grayling
through the ice,
1976 (Photo by
Erna Kantner)

through the winter, to June when there would be water again. Also, we had to have a few hundred left in the spring to cut and dry for emergencies and summer travel to the coast and back.

Some falls Keith and Anore camped at Paungaqtaugruk with their two little girls, Arunya and Willow. A couple times Bob Schiro, a young man from Connecticut, and Dorene Cameron, Oliver's daughter, camped there too. In those years the deep pool had to feed two or three teams, and we

Kole, Keith, Seth (kneeling) and Howard working on under-ice nets, 1976 (Photo by Erna Kantner)

all caught less, but it was worth it to have company for a season along our stretch of river. Keith was a meticulous fisherman, and because he liked humor he generally found some in whatever he did and shared it around. The girls jigged grayling, and times were good with friends on the ice.

Fall was tense and exciting with gathering and the abrupt change of seasons and method of travel, but something else besides darkness was coming our way: school. Kole and I didn't start our correspondence-school work until after ice fishing was over. But each day the catch diminished. Snow fell, filling in the stretches of jumbled ice, burying the grass and willows along the shores, turning the tundra white. The days grew shorter, the ice thicker, the holes harder to chop open. Finally, it was time to build a pole cache to put the fish up on, to keep them from getting buried and hollowed out by shrews; time to get the schoolbooks out at night after supper; time to set traps during the short days, and to start the dogs earning their keep.

brothers on the trapline

Morning darkness broke at eleven with a glow of orange leaking into the sky behind the Waring Mountains. The windows were opaque with ice around the edges. The thickness and spread of the frost gave the first indication of how cold the day was. My dad had the barrel stove going, and red ovals glowed on the sides. On the stove my mom heated left-over meat, and a pot of oatmeal made soft plopping sounds. Kole and I ate, using our same bowls and spoons from the night before, drank wa-ter out of the dipper, and then made heaps of our gear: snowpants and parkas, fur hats and mittens, mukluks if it was cold, shoepacks if it was warm (minus twenty or above). Finally we dressed in our overgarments and opened the door—always a big deal because the door had to shut again, and quickly. Cold air boiled in and turned to fog along the floor.

From outside we shoveled out the caribou-skin door and chipped away any ice that blocked it from closing. The edges of our noses tight-ened and started to freeze. The whole time shoveling we kept glancing over the tundra and out front on the river ice for foxes or other ani-mals, and scanning for fresh tracks. When the entrance was clear, we planted the shovels and raced slipping and sliding down the drifts to the dog yard. The wind drifts were ice-hard and smooth, and, unbeknownst to anyone except us, under that squeaky snow wound the labyrinth of our chipped caves.

The dogs were partially buried. They lunged to their feet, shak-ing off crusted snow. Shivering, they whined and wagged, nervous that they might get left home. The sled and harnesses had drifted over. Kole shook out the tow lines and the canvas sled bag and our battered apple box of bait and traps. I stretched out the lines and forced the frozen harnesses into approximate dog shapes, then hitched up the brothers, Bonehead and Murphy, first. We had just four dogs. More would mean more fishing. Besides, all our traps were close by. In those days, seven or eight dogs were a full-size team, a lot of animals to feed off the country. Unfortunately, our team included Flint, a ninety-pound malamute who ate every night but generally pulled only when there was something he felt like chasing, usually a moose.

We started off with me riding in the basket kneeling on a caribou skin. That meant Kole had to run behind, gripping the toprails to keep up and to steer the sled. The windblown snow dragged, grainy and slow against the runners. We traded positions without stopping the dogs. Running was hot, riding chilling. In both positions our faces froze. We headed out back, north into the wind, toward the lakes and sloughs on the tundra.

Our first trap was a 330 Conibear set for otter in a low willow cubby at a beaver dam. At the drift covering the dam, without command the dogs halted and dropped. They rolled and kicked their legs in the air, packing snow under their harnesses and slashing the frost off their faces.

Seth chops the teeth off a salmon before feeding it to the dogs, 1986 (Photo by Stacey Glaser)

Flint, in wheel position, was huge and brown and shed at the wrong time of year. He stretched back toward the sled, hungry, eyeing half of a *quaq* salmon, bait in the trapping box.

"Flint!" Kole whipped the sled with a loop of lead line. The big dog sat, contemplating whether snatching a chunk was worth a sapping with the lead-core rope.

The Conibear, a quick-kill trap, was wired to a buried pole and set with a piece of fish on the trigger wire and a nip of beaver castor nearby on a twig. There were no fresh tracks. The trap was partially drifted in. A gray jay had snapped the trigger but snow kept the jaws from closing. The bird's wings had scuffed the snow. I squeezed the bars together, quickly reset the trap, and scooped out the cubby. We climbed back on the sled and pulled the snow hook. "Get up there! Go ahead!" The dogs leaped up and followed the trail they knew by heart. The runners squeaked on the snow and we whistled and clucked encouragements.

The next trap site was off the trail, down a narrow path in the creek that drains over three dams just yards apart. The dogs' heads lifted; Bonehead's and Murphy's floppy ears rose. The team sped up. Sound carried in the cold. The dogs hoped for a fox or wolverine or any entertainment in the traps, or for what we dreaded and what excited the dogs most—moose towering in the trail.

Midwinter, and with the snow deep, moose followed our packed paths, punching holes and kicking up clods of snow. They weren't always inclined to step off it, up to their knees or chests. Kole and I gripped the toprails, expectant, nervous, hoping for a wolverine but afraid of moose, especially a cow with a calf. Our brake was poor, just two bent metal spikes. We carried only my pump .22 with its firing pin that often froze and left the gun more trouble and less useful than a stick.

The dogs clawed at the snow. Kole rode the brake. At the footpath to the traps I jumped off the sled and wedged the snowhook at the base of an alder. The dogs lunged and yowled. They stopped suddenly to hold their breaths, listening. Up in the tops of the trees we could hear wind coming. Again the dogs yanked at their harnesses, whining to go. Kole stepped over the tow lines and smacked them until they cowered and rolled their eyes at him. When he turned away, they sprang to their feet.

I followed the path into the willow thicket, down over the first dam. Holes marked where moose had followed this trail, too. The #4 double spring traps lay black and exposed, snapped. Unaware, the huge

Previous pages:
A cow moose
threatening to
charge out of
the frost covered
willows

animals had stomped the set. Tracks showed where a wolverine, too, had circled. The sign was fresh, still soft. I glanced around. Nothing moved except the tips of the tallest willows. I dropped to my knees in the snow, compressed the springs, set the triggers, and pushed the pans down to the right lightness for wolverine. My pockets held squares of white plastic trash bag, and I folded one around each trap and sifted fluffy snow over it. Then I swiveled and hurried back to the sled.

Past the slough, our trail jogged northeast near a beaver lodge. The wind was gusty. The dogs kept losing their footing on the polished ice. The sled slid sideways and flipped. We stuffed the spare traps and bait back in the apple box, and back in the basket. Beside us, lone stunted spruce bent in the wind, gray and difficult to make out in the blowing snow. I folded out the wolverine ruff on my hood and zipped my zipper

North wind drifts
snow off the tundra

up past the ermine-skin neck warmer. Kole did the same with his black-bear ruff. We broke ice off our eyelashes and shouted the dogs on. The wind got worse. Our faces froze in white patches. The stinging snow melted and refroze, crusting our cheeks and freezing our eyelashes together. We took turns walking in front of Murphy, an arm across our faces, the other mitten pulling his neck line, leading the dogs down the lakes. They squinted into the wind, grateful to have company out front.

The last trap site on the trail was protected by willows and spruce. Here, more than once in the past when I had checked traps alone, the team had dragged me across the ice toward a wolverine raging in a trap. I'd shot one-handed, gritting my teeth at each misfire caused by the sluggish firing pin.

Today, at the base of a big spruce, a lynx was caught in a trap. I shot it with the .22 while Kole held back the dogs. We stood under the tree, admiring the cat, melting our faces with bared hands. Once the animal was dead, the dogs lost interest and pawed crusted ice off their noses and bit the ice between their toes. I released the lynx's foot. Kole wrapped the silvery animal in the sled tarp while I reset the trap.

The trail home cut straight across the tundra. Snakes of snow whispered around the dogs' legs. Bonehead's testicles swung back and forth, black and frozen. It was getting dark. The southern sky glowed orange, fading to greenish, blue, and finally to black in the north.

At home we unhitched in blowing snow. Kole shoveled and chopped out dog food. I tossed two rock-hard fish to each dog and hurried to keep them at bay until I could help them with the ax, splitting the fish down the centers to make it easier to swallow the frozen chunks. I carried the lynx up to the drift in front of the house. Kole shoveled out the door and we bustled inside before it was buried again.

Our mom served dinner—boiled caribou meat—and then we skinned the lynx under the kerosene lamp. While we fleshed it with the *ichuun*, the skin flenser, and tacked the skin on a drying board, our dad expertly cut the carcass into meal-size portions. Lynx was one of our

A cross fox in
the willows

favorite meats, as good as luck-a-luck (whitefronted goose). And it was a break from eating caribou every night.

After the meat and skin were taken care of and the blood wiped up, we opened our correspondence-school books. We had started in November, after under-ice fishing, and were anxious to finish the year's requirements before the sun turned back to yellow in February. Trapping continued on until April. Soon after that the geese would return and we'd be hunting them and beaver for meat and skins.

By morning, while we were waiting for first light outside, the lynx skin would be dry enough to take off the board and to turn fur-out. We'd comb it, align the ears and face and tail, and in a few days the pelt would be ready to send out, although we probably wouldn't go to the village until we had a boxful to send to Seattle Fur Exchange. Kole and I were fortunate with the timing of our youthful trapping: as our trapline had increased, so had the rabbit, caribou, moose, and ptarmigan populations. Furbearers were plentiful, and for once fur prices climbed in time with their rise. The fur buyers were paying two hundred to five hundred dollars for lynx, sixty to one hundred and forty dollars for fox, and marten sold for as high as ninety dollars. In the villages, ladies bought wolverine skins for three hundred and fifty to four hundred dollars. We didn't bother the wolves and they were too smart to enter our cubbies and trail-sets. We never set more than thirty traps total, a few miles in each direction from home. Our expenses were little: a dozen traps every few years, thumbtacks, wire that we found and reused, a few boxes of .22 ammunition, four or five white trash bags, and a handful of nails. Kole was able to calculate the costs of necessary supplies better than I could. Even at this age, our differences were starting to show. More and more each year Kole read books and taught himself math and electronics, while I mushed the dogs and read animal tracks.

We didn't know what awaited fur prices, or that sentiment against trapping animals would grow. We also didn't know what awaited each of us as we followed our separate trails. Kole would be going to college, that was clear. I never suspected he might move to the States, of all places, and become an expert on that new invention, the computer. Or that I would own more than one of those mind-machines, too, and instead of trapping animals would take photographs of them, and send their pictures across the planet by tapping a few buttons. It was inconceivable that I, uninterested in words and poor at everything to do with them, would write a novel called *Ordinary Wolves*—that animal we didn't even trap. Inconceivable also that I could quit trapping completely, and still the land and animals would remain everything to me, and I'd find that I could not put my daily welfare before that debt.

iñupiaq mailman

My first memory of him is without sound, his brown face encircled
by his wolf ruff, peering in the door, shrouded in the cottony gauze of
a snowstorm. The swirling flakes hid his sled down on the river ice,
loaded with letters and packages he had brought miles across the tundra
and down the river from the village. Any stranger's or grizzled hunter's
face at the entrance to our sod home was a welcome sight, and maybe
that's all Harry Ticket would have been if his wife hadn't been postmis-
tress. During the years I was growing up, Harry and Sarah ran the post
office out of their house, metering out little bits of the world—welfare
checks and sweepstakes, catalogs and letters—to the villagers. My dad
told me Sarah had replaced a man who for a few months had had the
post office in his log cabin. But he took the stamp money and bought
bootleg whiskey and finished off with a free trip to jail.

Harry's job wasn't to deliver mail, but once or twice each winter,
when his house became crowded with our packages or he had a sudden
urge to hunt, he would hitch his sled behind his snowgo and break trail
across the miles to our place. Harry's arrival was like Christmas, only
better. It came as a surprise.

He was a heavy man with a respectable stomach and padded limbs.
Like many Eskimos, he now only walked when he had to. He loved his
snowgo and hunting with it. People hunted caribou when their meat
piles got low, but it was chasing and killing wolves that was a passion
to most—it brought prestige. In Harry that passion ran strong.

He would duck into our low, buried doorway, set down an armload of boxes, take off his muskrat parka, and shake the snow out of the fur. In those first moments his cold-stiffened face was expressionless, a mask. With his thick hands he would carefully sweep the snow across the hewn boards to make a pile next to the door where it wouldn't melt. I would quickly slip into my caribou socks so he wouldn't laugh at my grubby red feet. And then Kole and I might shyly nudge the mailbag and the brown cardboard packages to see what he had brought, to read the return addresses and imagine the contents and the huge cities they had traveled through.

No envelope would be opened while Harry sat at our plywood table. He slurped his scalding coffee and questioned my dad: "Wolf been come around much?" And Howie would run his fingers through his long, dark hair and glance into the surface of the mug of coffee clamped in his right hand. He had hunted and provided for Mabel Thomas, the daughter of an *aŋatkuq*. The wildness of the tundra and sea ice had captured his heart and made him turn his back forever on his zoology degree as if it had been nothing but a pinch of tobacco in the wind. He told us she had taught him to feel the land, to hear its voices. But that wasn't the sole reason hunters asked him about the wolves. Here, in this area, we were the only people who lived Out, away from the clamor and the barking of the village. The wolves wandered by as if our home were part of the bluff, which it was, buried in the ground and snow.

Howie trapped other animals for cash and fur for our clothes, but for reasons I didn't understand, he loved wolves, loved to see a whole pack stroll unafraid down the wide, frozen river, spread from shore to shore, or to watch them track down a moose, or just to listen to their howls wavering in the night. There was something he valued in them that I never valued when I was young. Their skins sold for more than lynx or wolverine, as high as six hundred dollars, and occasionally there were eight or ten on the ice out beyond where we tied the dogs. I always wanted to shoot three or four and have word sweep through the village.

Ravens teasing a
young wolf on
the ice

"Yeah, they showed up awhile back out in front on the ice," he
would say. I thought that if he and Harry switched places the questions
and answers would be exactly the same, comfortable yet vague and
noncommittal, the way people spoke in the village.

When Harry had finally rapped his empty coffee cup down and
thanked my mom for the food he seldom touched, he would say, "Well, I
gonna go check ta' country." Kole and I threw impatient glances at each
other. Then Harry would shake the glistening drops of water out of his
parka for a last time, grin at us, and call me Apakiilik, the Iñupiaq name
an old man in the village had given me; it had belonged to an old hunter
who had lived on this bluff earlier in the century. Harry walked up the

snow steps and disappeared, leaving us excited to open the Grandma packages and library boxes, yet somehow lonesome for people.

When we were little ragged kids growing up in the shadow of the Brooks Range, weeks or months would drift by between travelers stopping to warm up and have coffee and dried meat. People seemed to get farther and farther away as the light and sun shrank until the land was only blues and grays.

My mom missed people and light and the freedom of cars. In the winter she stared south at noon at the orange horizon and waited in quiet anguish for the sun to return. Our dad was from a city, too, yet that somehow made him love this silence more. Sometimes he told us about Toledo: the train tracks, gray buildings, a muskrat he once saw down by the river among the old tires. His stories were bleak, the wild animals missing. Erna didn't join in those stories. Her stories were infrequent and crowded with aunts and uncles and family.

Kole and I liked the land in our different ways, but in the long nights we read books and of course some of those books were about kids who had friends, and we yearned for some of our own. On those nights Howie sawed boards, read, or sewed a mink hat or mukluks, or fox mittens. In the twilight days we could persuade him to crawl through the snow caves we chipped out of the deep wind-packed front drift. I don't know why we spent hundreds of hours chipping caves. Maybe in the confining blue-blackness of our winding tunnels, caverns, and two-story rooms there was simply less space to miss people, and there under the snow our imaginations had the power to shape the world.

I think I was seven or eight when Harry arrived at our home on foot without a single envelope. He had burned up his engine chasing wolves and walked for hours without snowshoes, the fresh skin of a black wolf slung on his back. The long Arctic twilight was fading to bluish dusk when the dogs struck up a warning and he came slogging in. The exertion left him weak and shaky, leaning against the wall and the washbasin shelf for support. Under the glow of the kerosene lamp he looked haggard. I was surprised to see him drop the wolf hide to the floor without any flicker of triumph or acknowledgment in his eyes. And he had come inside without taking his rifle off his shoulder. People didn't bring rifles in at thirty below; the metal turned white with frost, and when the gun finally warmed up it was as wet as if it had been dunked down the water hole.

The next day Howie took him to Ambler by snowgo. They left in the morning darkness. Our dad's movements were short and quick. He worried a lot about breaking down and not being able to get back to take care of us. He didn't complain, but his scowl made his feelings clear. Wolf-chasing was at the root of it. He had wandered Alaska for years before moving to the Arctic to dig our igloo into the bluff and settle. This was as close to nature as he could get; it was where he wished to be, and he had an aversion to leaving and tried to discourage us from wanting even to go to the village.

Howard returning from checking traps, 1978 (Photo by Erna Kantner)

It was February, with the light still short and the snow deep. We didn't see him until the following night. No wind stirred the trees and nothing moved on the stark land. When he returned it was dark and we slid down the big front drift to meet him. His ice-crusted face was luminescent. He patted our shoulders with his wolverine-head mittens, and then we helped haul boxes of mail up to the glowing entrance of our buried home.

After we had scooped the tracked-in snow into the slop bucket and filled the barrel stove with logs, I sat surrounded by a circle of mail and, for reasons I couldn't fathom, still felt disturbed about Harry. Howie had warmed up, and he told us news while he cut hot meat out of the Dutch oven with his sheath knife. When Kole discovered that an order of D batteries had come in the mail, I forgot about Harry.

We filled the radio, and reception was good that night. An announcer's voice boomed into the dark moldy corners and drowned out the rustling of the mice digging in the moss behind the slabs. The huge outside world formed bright and clear in my mind. An announcer shrilled about President Nixon, and then a flood that killed hundreds of people, somewhere. We were allowed to listen to a few songs. For the first time I forgot that I intended to be a hunter and live off the land. The guitar music swelled in my head. I dreamed of being a singer and traveling to romantic-sounding places like Kentucky and Tennessee to be a real country boy.

After Harry's hard walk to our door we rarely saw him out of the village. He was nearing sixty, and life had been hard. He added on to his flat-topped frame house and had more room for mail to pile up. People stood around impatiently while Harry hauled the green-and-orange mail sacks down from the airfield and Sarah sorted the letters. When you opened their door to check mail you walked into a hot blast of caribou stew and musty clothes. Chubby babies crawled between the bags and peeked shyly from behind boxes. A few letters were trampled, but that rarely damaged the words inside. The bounty on wolves was rescinded. And cataracts grew across Harry's eyes and left the white tundra misty. The animals he loved to kill were finally just elusive shadows.

Harry was seldom friendly in town. His heart was out on the land where his ancestors had walked. He would sit on his porch, and when you walked up to check mail he would glare in your direction. "Post office closed," he would say harshly. Then he would laugh and say, "Too bad." He had a special way of saying it, *Tu-bat!*, that heated your veins on a fifty-below day.

When Jimmy Carter was president and I was twelve or thirteen, I presented Harry a snowgo drive belt in return for his having shot a wolverine in my trap that he came upon out in the country. I think he liked me after that. Howie said it was because I'd given him something and meant it. In the old Eskimo days people rarely gave to someone who had more than others. Because of Sarah's steady job, Harry had more than most and the village seldom let him forget it.

If I stopped to check mail he would rise stiffly off his seat on the porch and lead me into his house, right after sending some poor enraged person off with his head down and *"Tu-bat!"* tingling in his ears. Harry would pick up one of his fat diapered grandchildren crawling on the floor and hand him to me with the same aggressive thrust as if it were a package with my name on it, cluttering his house. "You have this one," he would say. "We got plen'y much." Back outside, I would sit near a sack of mail on the porch beside him. He would complain about whiteman junk, television and canned pop and CB radios that always burned out, and how he longed to be out hunting. "Where the wolves, Apakiilik?" he would ask.

And I would say, "I found a moose eaten, up the Nuna, near that beaver dam by the red rocks." We would glance over at Shield Downey's house, half surrounded by rounds of cut firewood. Shield had used dust from those rocks to paint his house red.

"If you starve, need ta' eat on ta' country"—he would nod and pause to see if I was paying attention—"blackfish, they always come by where the dam is open. Hold still for you. Otter and mink, you watch, they'll show you where." Harry liked to bring up the old ways. Things a hunter needed to know, things most other village kids wouldn't give a pack of cigarettes about. Those kids were embracing the world my family had turned its back on, and Harry knew that.

One night the north wind was roaring through the birch branches and shuddering our stove pipe. It was twenty below, and the wind lifted a wall of snow fifty feet high and five miles wide. Kole and I hunkered around the woodstove and studied civics in our correspondence-school books. I remember we had batteries that night because Howie tuned through the static until he found KJNP. Herbert W. Armstrong bellowed his radio evangelism into the night, raving about nuclear missiles and atomic bombs. I'd known about the bombs, of course, but the way he described the people and the cities and the destruction made me listen. The wind outside grew closer and louder until it rippled cold across my skin.

I laid my textbook on the wood box. I dragged out our tattered atlas and compared the colored countries: pink Russia to yellow America. Russia was huge. My mother told me the atlas was a relic and had been made before World War I. Borders were different now. She didn't look up from her sewing and spoke between stitches. I felt better.

Our door had drifted in by the time the lamp ran low that evening. Kerosene gelled in the cold, which made it harder to use, but we kept it in a jug outside because of the fumes. Howie cut through the snow with his machete and crawled out the top of our Dutch door to fetch the jug out of the drifts.

Although our dad's snowgo was buried under a tarp, Kole and I had dogs by that time; we could hear them barking. Out of the wind and darkness Howie hollered for his rifle. There was a *chink-chunk* as he chambered a round. Then he was shouting, his words torn away by the wind, and what he had thought was a wolverine clawing up the front drift turned out to be Harry.

Kole and I slipped into our parkas and overpants, climbed out, and shoveled out the door. We bustled Harry in before it buried again. When he took off his thick glasses his eyes were like black water holes in the ice; the light drowned in them, and none shone back. His mukluks were icy, and his beaver hat was crusted with snow. He curled thick swollen fingers around a cup of coffee.

He had been on a new snowgo, breaking trail from Kotzebue, on the coast 150 miles away. Ten miles downriver from our house, where the north wind wasn't strong and the snow was soft and deep, he had sunk into a patch of overflow—water flowing between the river ice and

the snow above it. The machine had foundered. It was a fancy new model with an electric starter, and the battery shorted out. Harry had abandoned the machine and begun walking. His snowshoes and mukluks became huge with ice, dragging like concrete in the deep snow. The last three miles he had been open to the wind that funneled out of the mountains. For part of that distance he had crawled. He nodded off beside the stove, and we laid out caribou skins for him to sleep on, below the little dirt and slab ledges Kole and I had for beds.

Harry's snores were loud, with uneven spaces between. I lay on my caribou skin and stared sleeplessly at the birch poles of our ceiling. The old spruce tree that grew just beside the roof over my bed was fighting for its life out in the wind. A root down near my head groaned with the gusts. On windy nights I used to lie in a sweat, petrified that the big spruce would fall, ripping the soil away above my cubby, letting the snow pack the house.

But that night I only distantly heard the wind. My mind flashed with pictures of Harry, weak and for the first time truly old. I lay on my back in the dark and summoned up past scary times. That huge winter brown bear our dad had shot time after time until it fell. It had been unable to hibernate because its worn teeth left it in agony. We made that couch out of its hide and would sit on it when our mom read us stories out of Kipling's *Jungle Book*. Then there was a rabid fox that snarled and foamed at the caribou skin on the door while Howie was gone with the dogs; in the end its skin was simply a warm pair of mittens. Compared to what I felt now, that kind of fear seemed small, almost friendly in its familiarity.

A mouse scurried over my face. I didn't flinch or try to slap it away. It seemed insignificant on its continuous search for a bite to eat, probably wary of running into a ferocious shrew but happy to be living inside. Even at that age, I had felt that life always was part bad and part good, marbled through like bear meat layered with fat. But that night seemed extra wide, extra dark and cold.

Previous pages: A traveler searching for the trail on the river ice

Men from the village came on snowgos before dawn. Howie shoveled the door out and talked with them. They drove on and chopped Harry's machine out of the ice, and hours later, as the morning darkness softened, they returned. We dug out our door again, and Harry walked stiffly as the men led him away.

I watched them grind up the river until the trees on the bluff hid them. The falling wind summoned up a few last drifts to cover the trail. I hitched up the dogs and mushed upriver, following. I'm not sure why. Maybe after I spent the night worrying over him, Harry had become more than the man who occasionally delivered the mail, a small piece of the outside world that entered our igloo. He was a friend, one who said few words and didn't laugh as often or as loud as he could have. As an Iñupiaq elder he stood on a melting ice sheet between a past and a future almost too swift and wide for him to bridge. What I couldn't imagine then was how hard it would be for me to make my own way.

The land was gray and quiet, not as powerful as it had been the day before. Maybe the change was only in me. I felt Harry going away, and it seemed as if he were forgetting something important, like his snowshoes or his rifle, as if I might be able to catch him on the trail and say a few words and my voice would snap him back to that hunter I had known. I felt there were things he could tell me that he had never spoken, that now I might never hear.

The bluff disappeared behind me. The high tundra where the trail left the river to climb over Onion Portage stretched in front. The team slowed in the grainy powder, weaving, and finally the trail was gone, the river only white waves of snow. I shouted at my dogs to go on, but they looked back and stopped. Far ahead I saw tiny black specks, and then they, too, were gone.

walking from barrow

Alvin Williams's grandpa, Nelson Greist, in the 1930s dog-teamed with his family from Barrow south to the Kobuk Valley. Young Nelson and his brothers and sisters walked beside the sled. It took them the better part of a year to make the journey, or more maybe. No one was counting days, nor did they travel in a straight line, but instead moved with the seasons and animals, hunting and gathering and following food. They had a hard trip, hungry times. Nelson's father died on the way, in the spring, and they buried him under rocks.

Nelson was a teenager, and he and his siblings and mother continued on, over the mountain range, down the steep Nakmaktuak Pass, down into the headwaters of the Ambler River. There, in fur garments and worn sealskin footwear, carrying firearms and few possessions, they came into the land of giants. Green ones. Trees.

These were coastal Eskimos, with eyes accustomed to scanning the vast and endless sweep of Arctic ice and tundra for animals to pursue and eat. They had come four hundred miles through low sloughs and lakes, brush and windswept wilderness, rising one footstep at a time with the land as it rose, into the rock formations of the Brooks Range. Beside them, mountains such as Mount Igikpak reached 8,500-foot spires to the sky, all the more stunning after the lunar levelness of sea ice and coastal plain. Now they were sliding down slopes into a claustrophobic rabbit-trail world of the forested Ambler River valley. Trees also marked the approaching edge of their traditional enemies' territory, that of the Athabascan Indians.

Undeterred, they built a raft, lashed on belongings, kids, and dogs, climbed aboard, and journeyed farther, floating downcurrent into a new life.

South of the Brooks Range, the family followed the Ambler River to the Kobuk, and the Kobuk to its mouth. They journeyed south to Selawik. There the Greist kids became adults and scattered to various villages. Nelson returned to Barrow by dog team, and back again to settle in the new village of Ambler at the confluence of the Ambler and Kobuk rivers. He married Edna Cleveland, a woman from Shungnak. Together they had nine children and raised grandchildren. Nelson built a house beside the Ambler Friends Church. He hunted for his family, trapped, found and cut jade; he worked for Louis Giddings, excavating at Onion Portage, and built that famous archaeologist a log cabin there, now a site on the National Historical Register. Being nobody's fool and noticing that the white people were clambering to the area around Onion Portage, Nelson claimed an eighty-acre Native allotment there in his wife's name.

As the years brought modernity flooding north, Nelson welcomed it. He didn't look back or wish for the old days. He had lived those lean times and didn't want to return to them, nor to the terrifying reign of the *aŋatkut*.

He built a large wooden boat and seasonally traveled to the coast to hunt *ugruk*, bearded seal, in the sea ice. After the hunting, after the ice melted, he fished commercially for salmon, camping with his family and beside his brother at North Tent City on the edge of Kotzebue. When salmon fishing entered a slump, he even tried his hand at agriculture, and for a few summers along the Ambler River he farmed potatoes.

Regardless of the relentless intrusion of the white world, Iñupiaq was the language the family lived. Nelson's English remained limited, intriguing to listen to, halting and sprinkled with seemingly random uses of the word *gonna*: "Gonna lotta caribou. Gonna run again." His voice was commanding and full of expectation that members of his family would jump. Around Ambler, Nelson established a reputation for being stubborn, more likely to lead than to follow, and capable out on the land. Out hunting, on the trail, he also had a reputation for never looking back. Maybe this was a result of his journey as a young man, maybe the old dog mushers only looked ahead, at their teams and beyond. Regardless, with the introduction of the gas-powered Snow Travelers it became important to learn this new skill, to glance back, even briefly, to check on fellow hunters, family, or even just the sled dragging behind.

Nelson didn't do that.

Before television, telling stories was an important part of Eskimo life on the land. Stories, and laughing. Teasing passed the time, teasing that often cut straight to the truth, mercilessly. Naturally, villagers enjoyed telling stories of this man from Barrow and making fun of his idiosyncrasies. Charlie Jones, an Iñupiaq hunter from the coast—famous for being a strong man and a mysteriously talented sled and boat builder—hunted with Nelson and grew tired of traveling the country with a companion who never looked back. Charlie would tell a story about trying to teach Nelson a lesson.

The two men were returning from hunting caribou in the flats across from Paungaqtaugruk. It was midwinter, cold on the trail, and growing colder as twilight fell. Nelson drove in front, the headlight on his John Deere snowgo carving a cone out of the darkness. Charlie followed, his basket sled, like Nelson's, heavy and bulging with caribou. Suddenly in the dimness he came upon a sled, caribou lashed on and still steaming. Nelson's sled had come unhitched from his snowgo, and, unaware, he had kept going, not peering back even once to check on it or on his hunting companion or anything else.

Charlie steered up beside the load, thawed his face, glanced around to note where on the river trail it was, and then he continued on. He didn't race up to tell Nelson. Twenty-five miles later, when they got to the village, it was dark, a cold north wind picking up. A good time to be home by the woodstove. In his huge hooded parka, his rifle across his back, Nelson bellowed, "Where my sled?" Charlie calmly stood up to the powerful man and his wrath. "Downriver. By Paungaqtaugruk. Maybe next time you'll try look behind."

In Ambler, in later years, Nelson was known as one of the few people who could navigate the trackless mountains to the north. He walked the country, traveled there by dog team and later by snowgo. He returned often, for years searching for the lost grave of his father. He never found it. It may be that when he left the grave he simply hadn't looked back.

Charlie Jones heading for the coast in his boat, 1974 (Photo by Erna Kantner)

His eldest daughter, Mary, grew up in Shungnak, Ambler, and Onion Portage, helping to haul logs to build the archaeologist's cabin. Mary Greist met Don Williams in passing during the winter of 1963 when he wintered there, and later Don built an igloo a few miles outside Ambler. They married, and Nelson's grandson, Alvin, was born in 1967, thirty years after Nelson arrived on the Kobuk River.

As boys, Alvin and I hunted to-gether with slingshots, carrying rocks in our pockets. By the time we got our first guns we were as close as brothers and without speaking could share shots with one rifle. Alvin had unbelievable eyesight. He could spot where a bullet hit a bear when it was still running. He could name which species of duck flew past—male or female—at great distances. His mixed blood worked in his favor, giving him height over many of his relatives, and a mixed-blood handsomeness, too. But there was never a question that he was Eskimo inside and out, with a handed-down hunger to hunt.

We both had dog teams: me, downriver surrounded by miles of wilderness, animals, and tracks; him, in town, going to school every

morning, playing basketball, watching America on television in the evenings, escaping on his dog team whenever he could.

Geese were our first passion. In May the night went away and they came, and it was a welcome trade. Sunshine and the sound of birds and bugs replaced frozen silence. We mushed across the land, the glare off

the snow cooking our faces while we searched for geese and bears and whatever else tasted good and had fat. Alvin was lean and lanky and happy-go-lucky, his teeth white in his darkly tanned face. Never far from our reach were our guns, and goose calls made from .12 gauge shotgun shells with the sides melted out.

Eventually we got our hands on snowgos, and Alvin was allowed to use his dad's aluminum boat with a 9.9 horsepower motor. We became not our parents' worst nightmares but something unexpectedly more frightening. With the introduction of cash, stores, mail planes, and the electric freezer, no one in the village would starve if we didn't come home, and we became part of a new village culture of technically en-hanced semisuicidal hunters. We did what no one else there, not our parents or Nelson, or even Clarence Wood, had done: we climbed on the shifting, crumbling Breakup ice and disappeared downriver. Gone for days, we dragged the boat from open lead to open lead, falling into

Alvin traveling on moving Breakup ice, 1985

the vessel when the ice broke under us. We ran reckless on rotting needle ice to retrieve geese, and we rode west on the pans when there was
no escaping ice jams.

Nights we hunted and afternoons occasionally stretched out on caribou skins and slept while herds of those animals crossed north around
us. We learned which ducks tasted best, which of their respective eggs
tasted good, and to shoot the female first so the male would come back.
We learned that otters came up once, beavers often circled back, bears
moaned like men when they were hurt and generally were more polite
than moose. We learned the look of the different ices, and how to thaw
out around a fire when we judged it wrong. Out on the land we brushed
shoulders with all the animals. All except one. One animal we never saw.

Clarence, squinting and serious, mentioned hunting them far to the
north. Nelson spoke similar stories to his grandson. And of course we
were bound to go searching.

When Alvin was twenty and I was twenty-two, we summoned up our
camping gear and courage and tent poles, and headed north to follow
some of Nelson's route. We weren't looking for Alvin's great-grandfa-
ther's grave, but for those creatures that had been mythical to us: Dall
sheep. Already Alvin was building a reputation as a sharp shot and a
hunter. I wanted to see these sheep and to taste their meat; I brought
along both rifle and camera. Alvin didn't have such cross-eyed visions.
He was there to hunt.

At that time, Kole was in college studying physics, and my parents had
moved away. I was living at our new igloo with my girlfriend, Stacey Glaser.
She came along with Alvin and me, unaware that this was not just another
outing with a tent and campfire. Stacey had grown up in Boston, in a mid-
dle-class neighborhood. When we met, she'd been living a safe American
life, with a car and furniture, working in a plastic-bottle factory, making
$4.10 an hour after four years with the company. Her people—her friends
and family—went to concerts and restaurants and followed the road; if
and when they camped, it wasn't camping the way Alvin and I did it.

Near the edge of the tree line we were already in unknown territory, glancing up draws and trying to memorize mountains. A valley invited and we veered north, into what turned out to be the wrong pass—not the Iñupiats' traditional route north, but a nearby one. The going was bad, the snow was ice hard, rough, scoured to sastrugi by wind. I drove my dad's old snowgo and dragged a heavy sled. Alvin had a brand-new Arctic Cat and had inherited the tendency not to look back. I had my own dislike of *turning* back. Danger we didn't count; we continued on.

Tired, and cut off by a rock face that obviously wasn't the route Nelson had traveled, we pitched our tent under a cornice. During that first night Alvin slept, while Stacey lay wide awake listening in fear for our impending death, convinced we would die under an avalanche. She elbowed me hourly as muffled explosions went off outside the wall of my canvas tent.

In the morning I was bushed and my back was hurting; Alvin was rested and revved to go. Packing up, we found the source of the night sounds: not an avalanche, but out in the snow Alvin's Coke cans had burst and left sticky streaks the shape of rabbit tracks staining the side wall of my tent. We lashed our loads, laughing about his lost soda pop. Alvin started his machine. Grinning, he gave it throttle and roared up the pass. Halfway up, the slope got too steep. He tried to turn. From the bottom Stacey and I saw a tiny snowgo begin to roll down the mountain. Quick and athletic, Alvin got it stopped, somehow, though now it was upside down. We watched the small figure let the snowgo roll one more flip, then restart the engine. He motored back down with a flattened windshield, unfazed, still in his usual cheerful mood.

Unwilling to turn back, we climbed to the top on foot, kicking and chopping footholds, longshoring his sled and our gear up and over the mountain. By afternoon, barely thirty miles into the journey, we abandoned my basket sled and left behind other things, including the spruce tent poles that we had been warned to cut and carry along.

At the top of the rocks we stopped. We stood in awe, possibly the way the Greist family had when they first looked over the mountains in the opposite direction and saw trees. North, on the other side, lay an eerie ice-cream world: white valleys stretching to the end of the sky, peak after peak disappearing into distance and mountains and more miles of snow-covered land. Stacey was a city girl—this was the moon. Alvin and I, lifelong Kobuk River boys, stood as if on the edge of a new continent, one we had never comprehended, a land where you couldn't build a fire to thaw out and couldn't chop new tent poles when you needed them.

We continued on, looking back, hoping the sky and land didn't breathe. Hours later, in the late evening twilight, we finally found willows large enough to lash together to pitch the tent. The ridgepole was low and leaning, and we piled blocks of snow around the sides for protection. Inside, we folded out the legs on my homemade five-gallon-can stove, raised the collapsible stovepipe, and built a fire from dead willows. I fried lynx meat, discovering that among other things we'd forgotten plates and utensils. We ate with our knives, joking about our hard trail, and then in the night after Stacey fell into exhausted sleep, Alvin and I thawed the wolf we'd shot that day and skinned it by flashlight.

The following day we left the tent pitched there. We left our sleeping bags and grub box, our gas cans and now, because of a shortage of gas, my snowgo, too. We continued on with just Alvin's machine and empty sled. We looked back more now, and worried about snow falling or wind burying the lonely ribbon of our trail to the tent and home. All the while we marveled at how Nelson, Clarence, and some of the Anaktuvuk hunters navigated this expanse without map or trail or any aid besides sheer knowledge. We found it hard to believe that the Greist family had made their way across this maze of mountains, and hundreds and hundreds of miles farther north.

Alvin drove; Stacey and I rode on caribou skins in his basket sled. The plan was to turn back when the tank neared half full. Sheep or no sheep, it would be over.

Across flats, far on the north side of the Noatak Valley, Alvin sighted small mountains with melted-out flanks. He sped up like a lead

Following pages: Looking north from the top of Cutler Valley

Dall sheep on a
mountaintop

dog heading home, the sled bouncing, his focus as narrow as a predator's. At the base of the mountains he stopped. We glassed the south-
facing slopes. Tiny ivory dots became what had been fable for all of our
lives. Two thousand feet up, near the peak—sheep!

We stripped down to pants and white wind shells and checked our
rifles. Stacey wanted nothing to do with racing up a mountain. As we had

left our gear miles and days back, she had been forced to abandon along the trail her definition of camping. Trusting and patient, she elected to stay below on the sled in the sun. Alvin and I were at the back wall of our world, no human sign here in the wilderness; we were young and tireless and in the land of mythical animals. We sprinted up the jumbled rocks.

Two thousand feet up, the slope flattened out. Rifles unslung, we stepped onto snow, yards from a herd of horned white creatures. There was no time to admire, to photograph, or even to kneel. They turned and with their heads high raced away across the crown of the mountain. We fired. Two rams dropped.

Alvin slid with the dead sheep down a snow chute, nearly vertical, to the valley below. I had to backtrack, hurrying down the rocks to find my misplaced marten-skin headband and meet him at the sled. There we circled the strange animals. We kneeled in the snow, admiring them and smiling at our luck. The sheep were furred all over like a caribou's neck—white hollow hair that was twisty and brittle. It left segments on our hands when we brushed our palms along their flanks. Their faces were fine-featured. Gnarled horns, with grain like curved brown hardwood, grew out of their white heads. Their feet too were vaguely similar to caribous', yet so dainty.

We cleaned the animals and then loaded them on the sled. We wiped our bloody hands with snow, shook off the red slush, and dried our fingers and the backs of our hands on our pants. Alvin put fresh cartridges in his gun, inhaled air from the chamber of his rifle, and smiled hugely. He glassed the valley with binoculars for other animals, wolves and wolverines, or brown bears. He dug in his bag and got out black whale muktuk his grandfather had given him—recently flown by airplane from Barrow. I unwrapped *paniqtuq*. Stacey got out chocolate. We ate quickly, recounting our trail to luck, repeatedly striding over to stare at the curly-horned creatures. And then, aware that storm or breakdown could still befall us, we turned and followed the long trail to our tent and the next day started home, gathering on the way all the things we had abandoned to get to that point.

Back in Ambler, Nelson was proud of his grandson. He asked for the sheep's lower legs, which he ate the marrow from. Alvin was hit by a speeding snowgo two days later. He was medevaced to Anchorage with a shattered leg. Good-natured and holding no grudge, he healed and went on to become one of the most capable hunters in the region, today living along the Kobuk, just up the hill from his grandpa.

In June when the birch leaves are babies, sparkling like green glass in
the all-night sun, Alvin buys an eleven-thousand-dollar aluminum jetboat. The ice has recently gone out in the river, and water—after white
winter—is a cached memory, an exotic highway to places of this season.
Irises, equisetums, and grass shoots poke up through the silted shores,
and mud sucks our boots as we stand admiring his biggest-ever new toy.
The boat is green and low and as unscathed as those pretty new leaves
that will fall in a few months. With a big ninety horsepower it skims the
water. Alvin's mother and his wife, Clara, want a ride. His dad wants a
porcupine to roast on his Kmart gas grill, which has finally melted out
of the snow. I climb in and go along for both.

The sun is warm and the quarter-mile-wide river growing swim-
mable for those who know how; none of us do, not more than a dog
paddle anyway. Alvin and Clara's two boys, Jeremy and Justin, have
come along and they face forward, joyful in the eye-tearing air. I glance
around the craft; there isn't a life preserver in sight. But, well, these
new store-bought boats don't sink, do they? We don't expect any problems or to see many animals, it being the middle of the day and the
middle of June. Regardless, Alvin has brought along a stack of guns.
June is when the animals and geese and birds disappear off the river
to the tundra and lakes to raise kids and grow new feathers. June in
the Arctic is a pivotal month, between winter—which is what we are
about—and quiet, leafy, buggy, unhunting summer. A boat ride upriver

now is simply expensive entertainment. Only autumn with its brisk air, rush of gathering, and the start of another winter will again quicken everyone's pulse.

A few bends above the village, I spot a straw-colored rump disappearing into the fireweed at the top of a cutbank. I'm surprised, because for the past twenty-five years, Alvin with his raven eyes has been the first to see nearly everything that moves. Also, you usually see a porcupine when you're not looking for one. We roar to shore and scrabble up the high bank and into the alders. Mosquitoes rise in welcome. After some maneuvering in the brush, I dispatch the animal local fashion with

Sunshine in the night along the Kobuk

Alvin's untried new yellow oar. I feel a superstitious pang of disloyalty to the land and wish that what reached between me and this creature had simply been a stick I'd picked up from the ground.

On the opposite sandbar we carefully lay the porcupine on his back and warn the boys not to kick sand. The sun is high, bright in the sky and on ripples of the lazy blue current. Grayling fin in an eddy behind the boat. It is slightly strange to be working on an animal in such warmth and sun: in late spring we usually hunt through the nights, and sleep into afternoon.

We slit the porcupine up the middle and skin the animal out, cutting it free at the wrists, ankles, tail, and throat. Alvin expertly splits the brisket and I the pelvis, and we ease the entrails aside. It takes two or three minutes. This, after all, is what we know, and a promptly cleaned porcupine tastes best.

Clara plucks a few handfuls of quills for beadwork. Alvin's mother, Mary, smiles. "Good boys. That's a fat one." We slip the meat into a Hefty bag and lean back on our heels, glancing down the water's edge and cleaning our knives. Alvin's gaze caresses his new boat.

For more than a couple of decades now, Alvin and I have cleaned our knives together. Our first forays out on water we used to paddle my dad's homemade kayaks, built with willow ribs and spruce stringers—light, light kayaks that we portaged across the tundra in spring nights, hunting meat, furs, and eggs. We mushed those small dog teams of ours what seemed like great distances across the tundra to see each other. In the village and downriver at my family's house, our friendship was founded on an unbroken chain of shared stories stretching back to the mists of our first memories. If we weren't silent because of stalking some animal, we were laughing, always, usually about old dogs, falling through the ice, or catching our thumbs in Conibears, adventures, and hardships that in hindsight were laughable. These days, Alvin works at Red Dog Mine, two weeks on, one week off. I drop in and out of college, always to return here, and he does the same. The distance between my parents' igloo and Don and

Mary's house has shrunk, with snowgos, fourwheelers, airplanes; those long days on the trail have been replaced by mere minutes, and the distance between Alvin and me has grown.

I stand and look at the brown plastic bag laid gently closed, the shiny jetboat, the red gas cans and heap of guns. The cooler full of Pepsi and turkey spreadables. The blue tarp. It is a good thing to bring home, an early summer porcupine fresh from feasting on fireweed and greens, but I feel the sheer weight of this technology that has come to carry our lives. How did the old Eskimos live before Hefty bags? How did Alvin and I even paddle, and run behind our teams, and snowshoe when these days winter and summer we ride and ride and ride?

The skin is spread on the sand, hair up now, clawed feet attached, furry chin high, eyes staring out over the water. My thoughts trail back down this little creature's last unlucky steps. Minutes ago he was nosing under the brush munching in the warm heart of an afternoon. Could my own complicated, desire-infested life cease so simply? What did his days hold, this stubby quill ball without aggression in all of a million ancestors? A friend from Pennsylvania once told me, "We club 'em when we see 'em." Why? I asked. "They kill trees" was the response. He didn't know you could eat porcupine. He thought I was a savage. Which is debatable, I guess.

Standing here on the sandbar with dinner in the bag and friends that years have forged into family, I feel at home and yet uneasy, too. Technology is tied up to the shore. Forces are out there and coming. Powerful things like pavement, and strip mines.

My friend splashes gas on the quills and I throw the match. The flat porcupine is a sheet of flame. Then he begins to shrink, pulling in toward some kind of forever, the head still grinning at the far shore of his life where he walked the earth for a time.

We burn his hide out of respect, I think—not for him, but for the big guys, the wolves and foxes and bears that might die badly if we didn't. Somehow we forget and don't think as often of the smaller animals: the weasels, mink, maybe the gray jays. We've seen our parents and elders do this with fire. We've saved the meat. We want to be respectful. Respect, though, here on the far edge of America, has grown to be a complicated creature that is nearly impossible to comprehend, and we all climb back in the boat and roar downstream.

sharpshooter

The photography virus infected me after I dropped out of college the
second time. Back at home along the river, rabbit populations had
crashed. The lynx had silently left for richer valleys. Wolverines were
absent, and, disconcertingly, even red fox tracks were scarce.

Around the place cache poles were rotting, squirrels had chewed in,
and my parents had moved away to find a place to grow food instead
of hunt it. They had left behind worn clothes, some of the tools, and
all of their furs. In the village, Keith and Anore, Ole and Sasha, and
others of my extended family had preceded them in moving south.
Dan Denslow and Pete MacManus had been killed in plane crashes. I
was unwilling to give up on my home, although I was lonely and not
certain what I was supposed to do with used sleds, old bear skins, and
my future. Thankfully, Don and Mary were like family and still lived
at the west end of town, and close friends Dave Fleming and Marcia
Kumamoto built a sod house upriver from Onion Portage and were living there. At the new Ambler post office with steel steps and an aluminum flagpole, my box was stuffed with ads and Cabela's catalogs selling
night-vision scopes and camo underwear; the small folded H. E. Goldberg and Seattle Fur Exchange price brochures were lost in the deluge,
and the fur prices they quoted were dismal.

Those banked dollars from my teenage trapping I'd mostly handed
over to the University of Alaska to teach me that I didn't fit in and
didn't know what I wanted to be. I'd come home to find that my career

Stacey picking
cranberries in the
fall, 1986

had collapsed: as a trapper I could no longer make the three thousand dollars a year that I called a good living.

Still, I gathered bait and boiled my traps with poplar bark, and roamed with dog team and snowgo, attempting to resuscitate my old life. Somewhere between the coffeepot on my campfires and cutting firewood and climbing mountains, I began to notice that taking photographs felt better than finding fox feet in my traps, creating three-legged misery in hopes of catching a nineteen-dollar pelt. (Unfortunately, I was still years from selling my first photo, to the *Bigfork Eagle* newspaper, for a quarter of the price of a rubbed spring fox.)

When fall came I was living with Stacey in my family's sod house. Her parents were hoping she would hurry up and return to the East Coast, or at least down to one of the normal states—preferably minus the jobless hunter-trapper boyfriend. From my perspective, we were doing daily what I'd been taught defined success: we picked buckets of cranberries and cut moss to reinsulate the igloo walls and patch mouse tunnels; we gathered fish for the dog team Bob and Doreen Schiro had loaned us and hunted caribou for our winter meat.

And still there was more, something achingly beautiful and bountiful and begging to be harvested: the huge sweep of crimson tundra rising to dusty blue mountains, yellow birches in distant dashes highlighting the tributaries, caribou in dark herds migrating from the north, brown bears occasionally out on the tundra near them, whiffing though not catching more than scent, then lowering their heads to eat blueberries again. An ermine lived under the woodpile. A hawk owl perched on the peeled spruce radio-antennae pole. Moose stood in the bright dying grass at the edge of ponds. Photography seemed a way of hunting and gathering it all—studying and conveying and capturing what I loved, with the plus of not diminishing the population of any species.

At that time, throughout the region, there were quite a few men in my position, high and dry between the old days of intense and important hunting and the new times of not needing enough meat to justify shooting everything that snowgos had made it possible to catch. And we couldn't earn enough from furs to afford the machines, gas, and parts. Much as we loved being out on the land, most of us couldn't find comfort here as mere tourists, either. This upending of the lifestyle had been going on since whalers came north in sailing ships, but the arrival of the snowmobile and the demise of working dogs was a major tipping point.

Some acquaintances of mine chose the popular route of becoming heavy-equipment operators at Prudhoe Bay, Red Dog Mine, and other sites, to stay in contact with nature. Drinking was another favored way of dealing with change, one that I attempted to master as persistently as photography.

Unlike alcohol, cameras were in my past and in my extended family. Lenny Kamerling was a photographer, and later a cinematographer who occasionally traveled through my childhood and my adult life. Anore Jones and Sasha Wik had always carried cameras, chronicling the country, albeit politely (more subsistence lifestyle shots of people and fish racks and less fleeing wildlife). And my mom had a compact Zeiss Icon camera that occasionally came out of the cupboard: when the house got extra buried by a big blizzard, when we launched a boat, or that winter Squint the muskrat moved in under the porch and started snacking out of the dog pot.

On my early photographic forays I carried the Zeiss. It was made back before World War II, in Germany, and had a foldout lens and a tiny first-ever solar panel, which acted as a light meter. Probably the camera was valuable, although because it belonged to my family I assumed it was recycled, hand-me-down, or found at the dump. The Zeiss had a focal length, of course, but I didn't know what it was and I wasn't interested in how that number related to my photos. Telephoto lenses and expensive equipment were heavy, for people with money, and would only slow me down. I preferred to keep things simple, and to save resources. Besides, I knew how to stalk. Shoot, I'd been hunting since I could walk. My family survived on what we shot. And after we shot it, if it was really fat and of course dead, occasionally we got out the camera; Howie stood up straight, Kole and I smiled at the fat, and my mom clicked a picture.

A bull moose was the first target of my professional wildlife photography. It was September, the beginning of rutting season. I didn't feel that I was starting too large; moose didn't always run away; they were big, and a camera had a big rectangular sight. How could I miss? And there was a provincial reason not to feel I was aiming too high: moose didn't receive credit the way caribou and other animals did. They were newcomers to the Arctic and not fixed in Iñupiaq traditions or appetites. Local people saw them simply as emergency dog food on the hoof. When I was a kid, when travelers stopped in at our igloo, we'd invariably ask: "See anything on the trail?" People who might have passed half a dozen moose that day but hadn't seen anything else would answer, "No, I never see nothing."

My chosen moose had antlers, tree-polished and ready to rumble. In hunter fashion, I crashed quietly through the dead willows and shallow pools along the edge of a beaver pond. The sun was low and behind me where it belonged. The lake was blue, with red-brown tundra spread behind. Farther off, the first snow frosted the Brooks Range. Already, I could tell photography was going to be a perfect addition to paradise. And no hunter worries about a crosswind or an unseen twig ricocheting the bullet, or warm weather ruining the meat.

The bull moose stood ankle deep (his ankles) on a swampy spit of land. I stepped into the grass and stopped sinking when the water was around my thighs. For a moment I weakened and wished for a 300mm lens to bring the thousand-pound animal closer to shore. But I had persistence, and hip boots. I sloshed forward and put him in the focus circle. With my local mind-set, I saw a moose as a large hunk of meat with a two-pound bone-armored brain, one that generally acted on a choice of three or four thoughts: chew, run, charge, and *huh?* You were only in trouble when "charge" came up.

I clicked a shot and then noticed my shadow stretched in front of me. It was holding a camera, too. I hunkered down to make it go away. Water poured into my boot. I gave up on the backdrop of those mountains and waded to the left, to a grassy hump with willows sprouting on it. The moose licked his lips. He stared and started down his mental list of options. Since it was rutting season, his list was a little shorter than usual. I snapped off a couple more shots and hightailed it away in great splashing leaps. I emptied my boots and strutted home across the tundra. Excited and hopeful, I sealed up the roll of film for mailing.

A week later a traveler stopped in. It was an Ambler schoolteacher, Nick Jans, another semireformed hunter who had taken to using his rifles less and packing cameras instead.

Nick had half a dozen trout in a cooler and was on his way home, boating upriver to the village. He threw his anchor in the weeds and came up for coffee. Nick was big and muscular and stuffed into giant camouflaged waders that seemed as if they could walk around by themselves. Ten years before, he had landed in Ambler as a hunting guide's assistant, a species the villagers loved to hate even more than they loved

A bull moose wading out of the river

to hate schoolteachers, the career he chose next. He came north hoping to shoot some of every animal, and did so—another feature not favored in a white guy by the Iñupiat. But unlike so many others, Nick had stayed, and paid his dues too, traveling the country with hunters, coaching high school basketball, and cutting wood for Minnie Gray and other elderly keepers of the old stories.

Now, exuberantly, he waved his Minolta around the stove to dry off condensation and told me about brown bears he had photographed the day before. Nick had shot nine or ten rolls of film. Listening, I dug in a drawer, dodging used and mouse-chewed Ziploc bags, searching for one to put my outgoing mail in—one miserly roll of 64 ASA slide film. A persistent little fantasy played in my mind: my moose picture in *Alaska* magazine. What did they pay for a cover shot? I could have asked Nick; his writings had already been published in that magazine and others. But I stuck to my hunter superstition: don't plan on and talk about caribou brisket, or boiled tongue, or fried heart before you go hunting.

A month later, after the river froze, Clarence Wood brought the first-class mail, as hunters occasionally still did when they were passing our way. The slides had arrived. It was late October but Clarence already had black frostbite on one cheek. I made coffee, and Stacey questioned him about the trail to town. Clarence rubbed an oversized hand through his cropped hair, ignored me, and teased my pretty girlfriend for being nervous about thin ice: "Com'on now, Daisy." We ate dried whitefish and bear fat. I wiped my hands on my jeans and opened my little green box of Fuji slides. The moose was huge and sharp and perfect in one of the slides—the one with a blade of grass across it like a great fuzzy spider leg. Clarence squinted through the transparency. He enjoyed a couple of big laughs. "Your picture in hurry," he said.

Previous pages:
Caribou swimming
the Kobuk

Sometime before all this, somewhere along the south shore—maybe at Onion Portage—I met Michio Hoshino. Michio was a young Japanese man with straight black hair that could have used a trim. He was friendly and nervous, and other than his soft hands, he looked like he might be from one of the villages. He carried a backpack that was half as big as he was, and unwieldy. When he got it off and leaned against a willow, he unlaced the top and pulled out the biggest camera and lens I'd ever seen. He pointed it at my head.

Michio was quiet and humble and had the ability to listen, qualities admired by the Iñupiat. Without really noticing, we became friends, and, because of my upbringing, I guess, I was more interested in that than in quizzing him about his career. Later, when I finally saw his books, I was awed by his bear and caribou and moose images and by his ability to capture not just one fat dead animal splayed in the snow, but the feel of the Arctic and its creatures alive and waist-deep in wilderness.

Eventually, I joined Michio in having more than a single lens. In sympathy and infinite generosity, Kole loaned me his new Minolta Maxxum. This wasn't a good deal for him, as I made his camera and lenses into fish tanks when rocks ripped open the bottom of Alvin's jetboat a few bends downriver from Nakmaktuak Pass. But that was later.

Clarence Wood (Photo by Nick Jans)

The first fall that I used Kole's camera was a good caribou fall. Thousands migrated by a quarter of a mile from the igloo, snowy mountains behind. Even at night Stacey and I could step outside in the endless dark and hear hooves clicking past.

The days stayed gray. I switched to Fuji Velvia film to get a drop on enhancing those bleak colors, a trick I'd learned from Michio, through Nick. Through Nick because I'd forgotten Michio's advice, too busy learning his recipe for spaghetti and listening to his story about a wolf appearing out of the darkness, staring at him across a campfire, then running away carrying Michio's brand-new Nikon in his teeth.

With the Velvia I headed back out. A relentless and gusty south-east wind scattered my scent in a million-acre swath downwind. I got frost-nipped hands and nice distance shots of running caribou butts. On the way home I warmed my fingers by running and waving my arms. I stopped suddenly and hunkered low, excited all over again by a caribou kill visited upon by ravens. They too promptly decided "no publicity today" and left.

Undeterred, I roamed the tundra daily. The north wind returned, whipping my manly smell south, away from the coming herds. I decided that the answer to wildlife photography lay in range. Most hunters, after a spell of missing their targets, develop a ferocity; deep in our fanatical little minds grows the craving to get *closer*. So I cut boughs and built a blind between caribou trails. Caribou flowed by on all sides. I clicked madly in many directions, learning one more lesson: spinning fast doesn't quite capture the effect of being surrounded by caribou.

On a trip to Ambler after Freezeup, more slides came home, from Kodak. I stopped in at Nick's cabin and we compared stories of the fall and caribou and encounters with bears. With our mutual interest in photography, and because we both lived year-round along the same river, we did more and more of that—relentless comparing of notes on the subject, drinking whiskey to lubricate our opinions, arguing over engines and approaches to writing, and showing each other our ever-so-gradually improving shots.

For decoration Nick had a bearskin mount slung over a beam and a shot-up alarm clock nailed next to his Nylon 66 rifle. On his table was a real slide projector, and beside it slippery photography magazines, granola bar wrappers, jalapeño sauce, and stacks of slides. Nick showed me images of distant brown bears—dead center in the photo—and of cow and calf moose. One of his moose shots was close to perfect. Leafing through *National Geographic*, I was properly jealous, and nodded yes to another glass of R&R. Unlike me, Nick had a job, and was not perplexed about the meaning of success. He had paychecks to invest in

Pentax and Minolta, jetboats and new snowgos, and because of that job and the accompanying toll of being trapped daily in a roomful of village teenagers, when he was out on the land he felt no qualms about thrashing his equipment in enthusiastic pursuit of what very often developed into a fleeing animal's ass.

Back downriver, I gave up on bovines, and good timing, too—the caribou were gone for the winter. Seventeen wolves filed out onto the river ice in front of the dog yard. I loaded my camera and hoofed after them, forgetting that Kole's Minolta wouldn't be useful if the pack decided I was a candidate to be a meal in the snow.

The wolves were not concerned with me or my photography; they walked unhurriedly. I slogged and puffed along at half their speed. It would have been a good distance shot if they hadn't been so far away. I came back to the igloo once again sweaty and pictureless, a kind of luck I'd known as a hunter, although not this consistently.

When the snow was finally deep and the trails in, I felt I'd learned some things. I was beginning to admit that having the right equipment might be slightly more important in photography than in hunting. You couldn't completely tough out a good picture. And animals didn't fall down after getting shot in the butt with a camera. I carried my gear bag constantly now, carried a longer and a shorter lens in addition to the 50mm lens. I'd switched the Minolta's shutter release selector off full-auto; I was learning that patience was part of the picture.

One day I was out running our dog team, on the first thirty-below morning. A wolverine appeared beside the team in a line of stunted spruce. He ran on short legs, exhaling puffs of frosted air. The dogs loved hunting. Bob Schiro's new pup, Pepper, leaped forward, tugging and hollering, his barking translating to: "Food! Food! Shoot!" The team lunged off the trail. The sled bounced over drifts and tussocks. Brush slapped me. I stayed patient. I got my camera out and shielded my face with it. The camera was cold and, like my old Remington .22, wouldn't shoot. I got the battery out and under my parka, under my

A wolverine climbing a
poplar for protection

armpit. I lost track of my glove and camera case, but the dogs were gaining on the wolverine. My fingers turned white. I was still patient. Somehow I got the battery back in. Then the sled caught on a small spruce tree that seemed to jump sideways to get in front of us at the last instant. My elbow furrowed in the snow, but I kept the barrel of that lens up. I rolled to my knees and shot fast, old hunter wisdom still in the way, strong and deceitful, taking over, telling me that a head shot was nice, but getting fur and food was how to feed the family.

The wolverine got away, disappeared onto the tundra—not a terrible thing for a shy creature who makes a living on abandoned bones. And me, I got one more crappy photo, one more reminder that whether it's camera, gun, or learning ice, all trails to being an expert are long, and the years would line up ahead.

Following pages:
A grizzly bear guards
his kill.

good-bye our season

Michio Hoshino
(Photo by
Don Williams)

In August a bear ate my friend. A brown bear, a Russian bear. Rain was coming down and cold when they told me: "A bear killed Michio in Russia." *Michio! My friend. Friend to half of Alaska.* What are words to tell of the vacuum of loss, the sitdown hollowness that loss pumps in?

This friend, Michio Hoshino, was the Ansel Adams of Japan. His photographs of Alaska played in our national magazines and touched corners of Japan I'll never know. His photographs were vast valleys, shoulders of mountains, stringy rivers cradling a lone animal in the land's arms. He made millions long to touch the face of wild land.

But here we didn't care about that. Here along the Kobuk River it took us a long time to hear of his fame in Japan. Here we liked him because he was Michio.

I don't know where I met him. I am lost trying to write his picture to strangers. Tonight all I can think of is that I hardly knew him. Most of us remember him forgetting things: mittens, his tripod, yellow blocks of Kodak film. He would arrive late, weeks—or a year—after he said he was coming. He'd say "Hi Sess," blink nervously, drag his camera bags into a pile, and mention that he came to photograph fall colors. Someone would point down at the riverbank, golden leaves stiff on the ground. "I'm too late?" he would ask, humble, polite. "Get in the boat," I'd say, not wanting him to disappear for another year. "Come down to the igloo. We'll see something." As if I knew. *He* knew. He wanted the leaves, but he knew the land after fall colors was the land getting ready for winter. Behind that humble smile was a genius for translating light on the land into emotion, into the hugeness of what is wilderness.

"Sess," he said. He rustled in his bags. "Tonight I cook."

"Sure, Michio, what are you going to make?"

"You know what is honeymoon salad?" I shook my head. "Lettuce alone."

He made curry that night. The sunset distracted him, and the rice boiled over. I moved to lift the lid; he nearly jumped over the table. I don't remember his words, only how fast he moved, stopping me from insulting the integrity of rice.

"I don't think I will marry now," Michio told me on a later visit, beside a campfire. The woman had to be Japanese, that was understood, and he spent a thousand times more time with bears and moose than with Japanese women. His book *Grizzly* was a family photo album of bears. *Moose*, an intimate panorama of the giants. And his later books, published in Japan, even more stunning.

"I'm thirty-eight. Too old to marry." He paused and blinked. "Sess, do you know what is a satellite bull moose?" I, who grew up in the wilderness, didn't. He told me a satellite bull was a moose that was too old, or too small, to fight the huge bulls for a harem. Instead he circled and waited, and when two mighty bulls crashed their egos and antlers and fought, there was his quiet chance.

"I hope I can be a satellite bull." Michio smiled.

A few years later Michio married Naoko, and the last time I saw him he carried a picture of a baby son so cute I wanted to steal the photo.

That was an August ago. He spent the night at our fish camp. Stacey and I and Michio sat in the tent and talked. He was writing something about us. I asked if his acclaimed essays were translated to English. He shook his head. "Impossible. They would not be good."

A week later, on the Kobuk River at sunset, he was waiting patiently for caribou to cross. I arrived with a boatload of Ambler friends. Michio stood in front of his tent, rice cooking, Nikon 600 f4 on its tripod. He joked with Mary Williams, saying he wanted to take her to Hawaii for her fiftieth birthday. On the north shore a line of caribou

waded in. Everyone hushed. The sun was fire boiling the clouds in the west. The caribou turned back and splashed to shore. "Oh," Michio said. "Oh, no. I came for this picture."

"You almost cry," Mary teased, Native-style, right on top of the truth.

The herd ran up the beach, no light in the north behind them now. I thumped an oar against the aluminum boat, an attempt to change the minds of a nervous and unpredictable animal, caribou. The herd ran back and waded in. Michio forgot us, forgot the world and his rice. The

Caribou crossing a sandbar

line of bulls crossed under the distant sun clouds. They swam bunched close, their antlers clacking together in the stillness. He switched camera bodies, shot more film, and finally stood. I'd never seen him so jubilant. He checked his rice.

And now, this fall. The Arctic summer fades and leaves the first stars, the first darkness since April. Inky rustling blackness. The memorial services are over in Fairbanks, Anchorage, Japan, and places I don't know. We sit close in our tents, our cabins, our towns. Near the light, we talk almost every night of Michio. We look at bears with different eyes. I've spent my life with bears more common than house pets, watching the natural terror of the food chain, and yet have never had a friend pulled out of this modern world, back into nature.

And now this fall the caribou come, the leaves float off the birches, the bears look for blueberries, and I miss you, Michio. I am left on earth feeling petty and stupid, worrying about the age on my hands, the people I want to like me, the ground squirrel digging under my tent. I don't know what that Russian bear was thinking. I don't know the whole story, why you were in a tent while the Japanese film crew and Kamchatka biologists were in a cabin. Why six men couldn't scare the bear off. I only know I miss you, my friend, and I will for a long time. I miss you like I would miss a season. And I know this land does not miss anyone, but if it did, you would be one.

Northern lights over the birches

124

flower of the fringe

Bob Uhl

On the fish camp spit of Nuvurak, in 1974, Bob Uhl taught me how to make rice. "Four cups of water." He paused and thought for moment. "One cup of rice." He was wearing hip boots, stacking salmon net with Keith Jones on the deep beach pebbles. I was barefoot. We stood in front of my parents' tent. Out back stretched miles of mudflats and marsh. Grass seed-heads bowed and glistened in the afternoon west wind. Down the shore toward Shield Downey's camp a dead, headless walrus was beached and stinking, sending a blubber oil slick angling out into the glinty blue water. Across Kotzebue Sound, a dark line of land ended in twin bumps that looked like smokestacks of a distant ship but were the White Alice radar towers, watching Russia.

I was nine and had lived up the Kobuk River below Onion Portage my whole life; Bob was that white guy we'd heard rumors of over the years. The one who came at the end of World War II to join the Alaska Scouts, a platoon of tough, rough frontier soldiers with dog teams. He'd married a native woman and faded into the Arctic to become legend. "Tat fella live more Eskimo than us," Iñupiaq travelers had told my family. I'd listened only to the part about this man knowing sea hunting: sea ice, fast ice, open leads, currents, seal hunting, harpoons, seal pokes, black meat—everything sea. Stuff we didn't learn upriver, didn't have, had to trade for. My parents, of course, had come from the States, too. My dad had lived with Mabel and Austin Thomas just a hundred or so miles up the coast from here. He had dog-teamed, traveled, and hunted the sea ice, but that ancient history, like Bob's, remained experience out of my reach.

Inside our white canvas wall tent, I put rice on to cook. My brother and parents were off pulling net. I was too little, no help. The rice took a long time to cook and came out different than expected. Bob was aged, bent even then. He should have known how much water to put with how much rice. And these days? More time has gone by, and that too has come out different than expected.

Returning from hunting caribou beyond the Igichuk Hills, I angle toward Uhls' cabin. Bob and his wife, Carrie, have wintered for fifty years there in a protective patch of spruce, out of the wind and worst drifting. It's five or six miles from their summer camp on the open ocean beach at Sisualik.

When I cross their trail, it's getting dark, blowing, snowing big flakes in the headlight of my snowgo. I drop down the bank of a frozen creek, then climb up to trees. Bob comes out in unlaced Sorels, terribly hunched and wearing that grin under his bright eyes. I'm reminded of a rare thing about this man: his welcome has always been the welcome of one who values a visitor more than his own day. Maybe the old Iñupiat taught him this.

I pull off my otter hat, my parka, shake the snow out of the wolf ruff, take off my binocs, untie a sack of caribou tongues and hearts for Carrie, and follow him. Under a buried lean-to I hear the throb of a portable generator. Inside, their plywood cabin is small, crowded, bright with fluorescent lights hanging from eight-penny nails pounded into the ceiling and bent over. The heat fogs my eyes. A kettle sings. A Canada goose honks and I start, then realize the sound comes from Carrie's bird clock on the wall, striking five. No wall escapes the miscellany of hanging calendars, photos, postcards, pins, Coleman mantels, mukluks, mittens, cartridges, cups. There seems no place to hang my overpants, sweater, fur hat, hardly room even to pile them on the floor. On the left of the entrance is a washbasin, on the right a honeybucket. In the middle of the floor is the big woodstove. Carrie sits on a bed against the back wall, smiling big.

"My Little Sweetheart! About time you visit!"

"There's hot water"—Bob gestures—"tea, instant coffee."

Both are three-quarters of a century old and more; they incorporate modern technology into gathering the old food, some of the vanishing few who still live Out, who know the old ways. Newcomers to camp life do exist—a tiny handful—yet they are just that, newcomers, more

A wind picking up along the coast

and more firmly plugged into seasonal jobs, the Internet, Sheetrock walls, frequent flier miles. The fine points of subsistence, such as what aquatic feed the pintail duck prefers to fatten on in late August, are irrelevant, forgotten, not noticed in the rush.

"You missed the *quaq* we had for lunch." Bob moves slowly, stiff, mumbles something about this winter's drought of visitors. I nod and blink, cross the floor to an old and polished schoolroom chair. My senses are numbed from the day of white ice, white land, wind, overflow, drifting snow, and caribou-like dots of distant shrubs on too much tundra. Bob and Carrie set out pot-roasted caribou pelvic meat that is dripping with fat, crackers, *pauṅgaqs* and *aqpiks*—crowberries and salmonberries—caribou backbone soup, cookies, and the fermented sourdock they call *quaġaq*, until there is no table space left. The table is plywood with a bright flower-print plastic tablecloth. The cabin is hot. Sweat sticks my shirt to my back. Bob feeds the stove relentlessly. He checks his cooking, edges Carnation canned milk and the sugar bowl my way. The carved spruce-root spoon in the bowl, and the way his huge thumb hooks over the rim, suspend me in the grip of childhood memory, seasons of visits and meals at the Uhls' summer camp.

Just now Bob is not saying a lot—surprising, for he likes to talk. But not that surprising, either. Carrie's guest book hanging on the wall reports only three visitors since the year began a month earlier. From my days of living alone upriver at Kapikaġvik after my brother and parents moved away, I remember the strangeness of speech after a hiatus, the struggle to make voice, corral feral thoughts, and shape the two into sense.

I sample the caribou soup. We begin talking about caribou. Bob knows more about the animals outside on my sled than I do. He explains that the young bulls' necks looked plucked because they continue to spar after the older bulls have dropped their antlers. He explains that the leg bones of larger bulls will be thinning as the marrow grows white and sweet and rich with approaching spring; pregnant cows will gain fat first on the back below the ribs, and will make better roasts—if the meat is not frozen too quickly. It goes without saying that he also knows in which season which hides will be good for parkas, *mamillaks,* and *qaatchiaqs,* in which month the *itchaurat* will start to be worth saving, why the lungs sometimes stick to the ribs, and a thousand more details of this single species, caribou.

His knowledge is vast, impressive, not quite astonishing.

Most folks hunt caribou here in northwest Alaska. The law says we may each shoot five per day, every day of the year. Over the course of a lifetime people eat plenty. A scant few still sleep on caribou hides, wear a skin garment or two, pay some attention to flavor.

What's surprising is Bob's affiliation with the daily goings-on not only of this staple food animal, but also of a thousand more of Earth's tribes: the widgeon, swan, gray jay, beluga, lowbush cranberry, wolverine, west wind, wolf, storm-warning waves, cirrus cloud, fall ice, spring ice, new ice, thin ice, raven, fireweed, willow, aspen, flint, obsidian, ivory, eider, otter, *ugruk.* For each, his experience encompasses the tastes and tools therein—seal oil, seal-oil lamps, sealskin mukluk bottoms, sealskin rope, seal-intestine raincoats, seal intestine braided dried eaten. Subsistence in this home permeates all. The paradox here is the extent to which gathering information has transcended simple food collection. Wingspans. Life spans. Famines. Patterns. No minutia of nature, it seems, has eluded Bob Uhl's inquisition.

Glancing around at the heaped clothes and clutter, the sheer lack of space created by the concentration of this lifestyle with its focus on survival, I find the idea of writing more than a note inconceivable. Yet Bob has made the extra effort over the years to write down a portion of his knowledge. In the 1970s, the National Park Service asked Bob and Carrie to research and write *Tagiimsinyakmiit,* a comprehensive manual of subsistence living patterns in Cape Krusenstern National Monument. And in 2004 their decade-long journal of animal, weather, and land conditions, *Daily Observations from Sisualik,* also was published.

However, Bob saves his most passionate written words for the fragile gentian flower.

The wind gusts in the treetops. Big flakes swirl down outside the window. We hunch on firewood stumps under the harsh fluorescent light, drinking Lipton tea. Living these past few years across Kotzebue Sound, in town, I'd forgotten the hunching of tent life, cabin life, and sod igloo life—hunching on Blazo boxes, near the table, by the stove, on the edge of a bed. Hunching waiting for animals to approach. The years show this in Bob's shoulders. The years inexorably press them forward and down, toward the earth.

Now he puckers his lips, thinking. Lines in his face divulge the story of half a century out in savage Arctic conditions, constant hunting and gathering beside and beyond the holler of hunger. And Carrie, more: eighty years out here on the land.

I slice one more bite of meat and good fat, thankful that I can appreciate their *niqipiaq*. This is important. And though my knife is homemade, my parka sewn by me, my life started and spent in the Arctic too, I feel immature, inattentive, unlearned. It's an insecurity some of us bear, we the children of changing times on a frontier falling apart. It is hard to look Bob in the eye. Impossible to debate him. Nodding has been my wisest comment. In the silence my mind wanders. I spoon a bowl of *quaġaq*. The tea is good, the water melted lake ice. I wonder, will the conversation turn to his passion, his unusual friend? On visits before tonight we've talked of this flower he's devoted to. I've photographed it for him, nodded, agreed, and still am no closer to comprehending. I don't get it. I struggle enough attempting to describe my friend, let alone his friend from another kingdom. That remains his story to write.

How many important things do we miss as we go pell-mell through life, from day to day pushed by those chores we believe imperative to our existence? One cannot deny the necessity of meeting our own physical needs, those of our family, and sometimes of our neighbor. However, it seems most of us are so intent on these that we pass unaware some aesthetic treasure that in itself can make the hardness of living worthwhile. So it was with me, following the daily challenges of life for thirty years, bypassing a treasure that, once I recognized it, I could not then imagine life complete without it.

The treasure is a purple-blue flower on a fragile salt-marsh plant. This flower lives just one place on American soil, one narrow coastal strip of land above the Arctic Circle. Part of this zone of occurrence is our back yard in Sisualik, a sand-gravel spit on the north shore of Kotzebue Sound.

It seems unthinkable now that for so many years in pursuing a subsistence life, I could pass or even trample this jewel underfoot. Life—or making a life—in those years was very intense and left little time for aesthetic concerns. So far as we know, this wild plant species is not eaten by any creature, is not used for shelter, serves no utilitarian purpose. Appreciation of it involves the spirit—beauty, design, color, and perseverance—not practical usefulness.

There is, however, much more to this plant than meets the eye. The part that does meet the eye, for only a week or ten days each July, has a mesmerizing effect on me. The budlike flower with a light green base and four sharp fingers holding fast to the near-luminescent purple-blue petals has a beauty that cannot be described adequately with words. The delicate tubular blossom opens for one or two sunny days to reveal pistil and anthers—opens so briefly and unexpectedly that one might think the plant dares show off its deep inflorescence only before the much paler summer sky. In spite of this short, shy exposure of secret parts, the cycle of life is completed. The color of the petals quickly fades, the seed completes its maturity, and the whole plant becomes straw colored and again anonymous in the chaff of the salt marsh.

The exceptional nature of survival of this fringed gentian has caused me to focus attention on this bit of life and form a relationship with it that is hard to explain in words to another person. What kind of relationship can one have with a plant? you ask. I would reply that maybe quite a unique relationship can develop. I say unique because it may be unique to me.

Animals develop close relationships to plants on a nutritional level. The caribou must have his lichens, the moose his willows, the bear his berries. These attachments are easily recognized. Perhaps man is unique in being able to have a more spiritual rapport. After looking for, anticipating, and watching this remarkable flower for many years, I find that at any time during fall, deep winter, or early spring I can close my eyes and visualize these gentians: the beautiful color, the attractive form, and even the erect, defiant stance the plant seems to take against Arctic gales, floods, and early frosts or snowstorms.

"Well. How did your caribou look?" Bob asks.

"Pretty good." I mutter, joking, "till I started shooting." I'm not sure he hears. "I got a cow, and a couple bulls," I admit warily.

"Hmmm." He nods, makes no comments. Again I get a flash of suspicion that he already knows everything I might say. I briefly describe my mile-long sneak through deep snow. He has already noticed that I left my snowshoes at home. The telling feels wrong. It does not mix well with hunter humility, a tradition we both wear with our skin. But he will press for details, banking them the way so many gather and bank dollars. Also, I include this information knowing he is one of very few hunters in this region who, like me, feels less than comfortable with this new practice of chasing down animals with machines.

I admit that my stealth was better than my shooting. Bob grins. Carrie listens to our conversation, yet also to the AM radio, the VHF, awaiting the ring of their camp phone—electric boxes that connect her now to a different pulse of the planet.

I sit at their heaped table, comfortable but feeling trapped. Beside my shoulder the disarray on the wall mirrors my mind, yet offers consolation; a note card is penned with the words "My life has been the poem I would have writ, / But I could not both live and utter it.—Henry David Thoreau." Above the table an aged yellow napkin reads SKINNY COOKS CAN'T BE TRUSTED.

The trapped feeling comes because here in our region crimes—time in jail, even—carry no stigma compared to bringing home skinny meat. These elders could use meat. And I hit the fat cow in the guts, and the large bull only slightly better. I can't give them an animal less than perfectly shot. I have to give them the smaller bull, which will be the least fat of the three. Worse, in haste, with the wind rising and the horizons vanishing, I'd cut the bony lower legs off the bulls and left them for the foxes. Bull *patiq* bones are Carrie and Bob's favorite. How could I be so thoughtless? Bob and Carrie's food from the land has always been of sterling quality. There is no compromise. This requires an intense amount of an almost extinct element: respect. Respect, that forgotten forsaken unromantic reality; taking the best care of what you harvest is the valorous fundamental of harvesting.

Nowadays, snowgos crisscross the tundra around their cabin. Hunters raised on machines and video games chase down furbearers, and much of everything that moves, counting coup with the numbers. Hunting no longer can be said to make livings; livings are made to hunt.

We drink more tea, talk about rice for a while. Jasmine rice, according to Bob, makes great rice, not such good caribou soup. Plain white rice is better for that. I mention basmati rice. It comes in a little burlap bag, from India, I think, via Costco. Our rice conversation eddies for a time around Michio Hoshino, the Japanese wildlife photographer a brown bear took from us, a friend we both miss. Outside it is black by now, blowing snow. My home is miles across tundra and frozen ocean that tonight, in a thirty-knot wind, will look pretty much the same up, down, and sideways. Also, there is overflow—water under the snow— out there somewhere, dangerous. I decide to spend the night, what they have been requesting since I came through the door.

Bob and I talk while I eat bowls of mixed *aqpiks* and *pauṅġaqs*. He explains overflow and ocean currents under ice, strangely affected by wind even in winter when the ocean is frozen over. Carrie overhears someone on VHF, from a house in Kotzebue, selling a wolf skin. Three hundred and fifty dollars. The static coming out of the small white radio pierces the cabin, the volume so loud my teeth ache. Bob talks on.

"Shh! Bob!" Carrie commands. This is not simply news. A substantial percentage of the residents of the region are related to her. Apparently the seller is from the village of Noorvik. An unpleasant-sounding woman's voice blares, demanding, "What color? Black or gray?" Static and voices rip the room, prompting images in my head of Iñupiaq homes in Ambler, Kobuk, Kivalina, and other villages.

"Gray one," Carrie translates for us. The price drops to two hundred and fifty dollars. She flips on AM radio KOTZ in Kotzebue. A careless-voiced sixteen-year-old kid is announcing tonight; Carrie's not impressed with his lack of reverence for the elders' choice, gospel music. She snaps it off.

She tells me of two wolves they've heard this winter, howling up the valley. The wolves, she says, were killed by a friend, yesterday. The man called Carrie on a handheld VHF immediately after chasing down and shooting the animals.

Earlier today I'd seen the skinned carcasses at the top of a pass, beside a snowgo trail. Bob chuckles, mentions that fat wolf is better eating than skinny caribou. This starts him on a new line of questioning. Where had I been? Where were the wolf carcasses? Where did I first spot caribou? Where exactly? He rains words and place names on me. Situkuyok River, Sivisok Slough, Napaktuktuk Mountain, Aukulak Lagoon, Nauyauruk. *Exactly*, to Bob, does not mean somewhere behind those mountains. It means beside which shrub in the million acres to the north did I find meat?

He shows no chagrin at the death of these wolves. He showed none a few years back when the first marten he'd ever seen came through these hills, set up housekeeping here in the spruce, and became his newest tutor—until young men came and killed it. There is no malice in his voice. After all these years, not a shred of disappointment. I realize I will have to ask him how he keeps his humor and hope. I need some of his wisdom, and peace. Every week or so some hunter tells me in gloating detail of chasing down a wolf, or three, seven, a whole pack.

I back away now from my vituperous thoughts, marvel again at this man's temperance. How he cherishes each phalarope, each seagull, each red fox, moose, grizzly, each gentian seed whose path crosses his.

Those who delve into the mysteries of this successful form of truly wild life find that it thrives in the harshest of environments and is an annual in our area, one of few Arctic annuals. It must grow from seed, come to flower, and produce seed all in a condensed summer. This is its total life.

Quite by accident one year, through a chance photograph of a plant right in camp, we learned that seed might have lain dormant for eight years before another plant appeared on that exact spot. This seemed a miraculous resurrection of life. What magic for maintaining existence is in that almost microscopic seed?

The fringed gentian, commonly called saved gentian, has small weak-looking roots, a thin sturdy upright stem, and a few narrow light-green leaves. It does not appear to have enough root-feeding or photosynthetic equipment to produce the large terminal flower that is the glory of this bit of Arctic life. Its numbers vary much from year to year in our location at Sisualik. There can be hundreds, even thousands some years, while in others a single plant is difficult to find.

All this is no excuse for my living with the plant for thirty years without ever noticing it. Nor am I excused because its spectacular blossom is obvious in that form for just a few days each summer.

I will be eternally grateful to a friend who one day stooped to point out what I had not seen for myself in these many years of walking on the spit of land in pursuit of various things to sustain our life. It may be that this is what friends are for. He did not know the full name of the plant but recognized it as a gentian. Once I had seen the perfect blend of petal color, I wanted to know more about this flower bud that I assumed, at first, must never open to the outside world of pollinators.

Even more odd was a bit of information a botanist later told us: the nearest place to our Noatak Delta/Baldwin Peninsula that this plant is found is the delta of the McKenzie River, a thousand miles up the coast in northern Canada. Why such odd gaps in its circumboreal distribution? Why is it not found in the Eastern Siberian Arctic nor on river delta areas in the sub-Arctic south of Kotzebue Sound?

These questions and other mysteries add to the attractiveness of this plant living, and making a success of living, in a zone at the northern edge of the habitat for most plant, animal, and fish species. In its own vascular plant world, it joins caribou, Dolly Varden, and Eskimos as forms of life that can thrive on the very edge of conditions that seem to prevent other forms from existing.

Because the plant seems so fragile and its numbers vary so, as I grow older in years there seems a certain parallel of plant with human life. Will we meet again for that short week at July's end? Will I survive another winter to be there for the meeting? Will this be the summer that no plant of this species raises its most beautiful head above the marsh grasses of Sisualik?

The lights flicker. Bob and Carrie turn to each other, question at what hour he filled the generator, when the light will extinguish.

"Bob always get me any kinda furs, all those years." Carrie is up from the bed, shoving dishes around. Her wrist hurts her; cutting even bread is painful. Spending the night here reminds me of forgotten details, such as serious pains and sprains that never see a doctor, the need to not take up extra room, to not use extra cups of water. This evening brings back the times of listening to stories (nearly always of the land), not requiring entertainment to be entertained.

Carrie laughs. She's still thinking about wolves. "He hunt better than all of them, but he never get me wolf. Here this time I thought he's going to get me wolf."

"Well." Bob starts to feed the stove and changes his mind. He seems to lose his train of thought and momentarily stands staring out the small high window. Again, I think I recognize a shard of myself in his movements—myself at Kapikaġvik, pleased to have unexpected company yet nervous around people, repeatedly feeding the fire, shifting the kettle, heating water, offering coffee to a guest already holding a mug. And something else, something I hardly recall yet miss so much about living Out. Could it be valuing every human more because of the daily lack of society? Bob resumes feeding the fire. He raises a stick of firewood in his hand. He half-kneels, lowering himself stiffly to the mouth of the stove. "Carrie, you know the wolf is a fellow creature of mine. The polar bear, too. I've never shot either of those creatures, and it's unlikely that I'll start now."

Their exchange is humorous. Bob is old, gray, stooped, no tooth anywhere in his smile. He wears a plain white T-shirt. His arms and hands are huge, young-looking and powerful. His bright eyes are the eyes of a naturalist born in California when Hitler was an unheeded young complainer, Hoover our president, Henry Ford the future. A naturalist taught to be Eskimo before most humans on the planet were born. Taught by the Old People, the last of the few who remembered the remains of what being Eskimo once meant. The sheer knowledge and experience leave no question in the night. If this elder decided to hunt the wolf or polar bear, the land would open to his hands.

When one first becomes acquainted with this Arctic beauty, given its fragility and vulnerability in the harsh habitat that it chooses, one believes that it exists on the very edge of oblivion, a species endangered by its own choices. It is, remember, an annual. Its chosen habitat is where a large river delta meets an often violent Arctic sea. Marine flooding, when temperatures are far below freezing, can cause the formation of a salt-saturated liquid deadly to all vegetation. Also, freshwater flooding from the river system is a periodic event both in the ice-free portion of the year and after ice formation. Temperatures can fluctuate from negative sixty degrees Fahrenheit to as high as eighty degrees through the seed and growth period.

At one time, it seemed to me that even a few random meteorological circumstances could bring about the extirpation of this fringed gentian. I was unaware that this fragile life-form had hidden virtues that compensated for its apparent vulnerability.

Those virtues are in the indestructible seed. A severe environment is needed to spark the near microscopic seed into germination. Soaking, maybe in salt and fresh water, freezing, maybe at very low temperatures, then soaking again at high early spring meltwater temperatures—this seems to be the combination that unlocks the life trapped in the seed.

Earlier I suggested that a relationship had developed between this unusual plant and me. What kind of a relationship could that be? One would think it would have to be pretty one-sided, and perhaps it is, but then we may not know all there is to know about relationships between the various forms of life. From my side, I do know that each late June or early July, I develop what I can only call a heartache to see the first pale green shoots pointed like a spear that will prove that there will indeed be a fringed gentian to see again this growing season.

The heartache also comes in part from long dark winter months when one wonders if the sun will come back again with its warmth and light and life-generating rays. Amid those thoughts a luminescent purple-blue image with delicate angular lines and curves appears in the dismal darkness and one finds a broad smile spreading and wiping the countenance clear; the sun will return and there will be gentians to be seen!

Fringed Gentian
(*gentianopsis*
detonsa ssp.
detonsa)

The generator is off, the cabin black. "Well." Bob is somewhere in the blackness, near the table, still talking. "Thanks for the conversation."

And I could cry in the dark on this iron cot. I visit Bob and Carrie when I can. I try to listen. It is hard with my big mouth, poor memory, and cluttered thoughts. Often in desperation I fear the only thing I'll remember clearly about them is that Carrie has always called me Little Sweetheart and Bob was wrong about the four cups of water. Lying here in the dark, I have trouble believing what has happened to the way of life into which I was born. Subsistence has melted in our hands. Living off the land, how did it drip away? How could the cash and computers, the canned food and machines, have taken so much, left so little? So many of us trusted that we would be true hunters but learned only how to kill, never made it anywhere close. We wander instead, adrift yet chained to the conveniences and cardboard-wrapped contraptions. The old life has vanished. Bob and Carrie lived that life, breathed the land, and walked from that past, carrying their mukluks and parkas and belongings into this twenty-first century.

And now I'm falling asleep. Here in the dark in their presence, I recognize a tenderness, a bottomless respect for the creatures and creations of the land, and I have no idea what to do with that recognition.

Darkness—huge and boundless, with only my one scoop of light, which thins across snow to gray, grayer, blackness. No assurance out there of another human, not on this planet, anyway. I shovel my cave by head-light. Pitch in twin sleeping bags, a caribou hide, food. It's small inside; big out here, and silent, a few flakes coming down, and a few stars blurry up there and not sharing their hard-traveling light. The air is not cold, only sixteen below, but a north breeze sears my cheeks.

The Darkness is a heavy tarpaulin across the shoulders, a blackness inside my skull, extra gravity camped in every cell. I'd like to say it's exotic but I have lived in the Arctic too long. It's not. It's an old friend, and an enemy too; a price to be paid.

Summer is sun. Something has to give for a thing as amazing as sun all night. Sun so sunny your brain can't accept that it could ever all go away; so sunny that the days are like science fiction—or just our old interesting earth.

In the dark I pause my mental candlepowering, listen. The flakes make faint whistling sounds falling on their kin, or is that imagined? In the distance I hear sharp clattery reports, teenage moose practicing what they recently saw their elders practicing. I press the switch on my LED headlight. It refuses to turn off. The switch must have been made and tested somewhere warm and doesn't appreciate cold.

I frame the opening with my snowshoes, cut blocks of snow to shield the entrance. Darkness has a predictability. Wind? Well, on the

tundra, wind does, too, an unpredictable kind of predictability: this silence could vanish into roaring and drifting storm all too quickly. It will. Darkness, on the other hand, faithfully follows the clock.

Daylight is spiraling downward. Night beginning at 4:00 p.m. will fade back to light by 11:00 a.m. In a snow cave, in midwinter, you can go crazy without a timepiece. Once, out photographing moose near Sivisok Slough, I had the flu but no watch; my bones hurt and I quit digging too soon. My feet fit in the bottom of the cave. My head stuck out. Rising wind sifted snow into my sleeping bag. I huddled and hallucinated, writhed and agonized, for seventeen hours: 5:00 p.m.? Midnight? 10:00 a.m.? *What kind of hell night is this?*

Now, under the cone of the headlight I smile at my old joke about a snow cave's virtue. Not a joke, just a threadbare quip: *Stormy weather, snow cave you can piss into the wall, tent you can't.* I put my glove over the light, inhale stillness, listen longer to the moose mock-battle off in the Darkness.

At the north shore of Kotzebue I kill my engine a hundred yards out onto the ice. All people and machine tracks have ceased. Behind me snowgos spark and clatter down the city streets. Ahead is the channel, deep, swift, and potentially dangerous. On the ice, I pause and take a few photographs, then retie my camera pack to the snowgo and unsheathe an ax. I walk, stopping every ten steps or so to test the ice. Yesterday an elderly friend asked if I'd make him a trail across the sound, to the hills behind Sisualik. Today that is my excuse for traveling on thin ice, hunting photographs and visiting four-legged friends, a combination I've grown to enjoy.

After all the cities I've had to travel through lately, I'm restless to get away from town, to the open tundra. Ahead, past a strip of glare ice, the rest is smooth, all the same color, with the same amount of snow and frost, meaning that this area probably all froze the same night. It is uniformly thick, six inches and more. The walking is nice, with my back to town and in front of me the endless fling of white stretching away to the hills and off to the west toward Siberia.

In half a mile I make it to the far side of the channel, to jumbled ice over the sandbar. I jog back, retrieve my snowgo, and drive northwest heading across new ice. Refrozen fissures and occasional caribou trails flash under my skis. The trails head east. None that I see are human. It is exhilarating. Even with the sun leaving, I like this time of year. The general idea in early fall crossings is that if the channel is safe, the

shallow estuary will be safer. That's the idea, but you're driving over fifteen miles of brand-new ice, alone, and most of the muscles in your body are aware of that.

Kotzebue Sound glitters, flat and white and frosty. I stop to check patches of pale green overflow. There are miles of ice behind me now, too. At the far shore, I angle up the ridge to the tundra. Caribou have been here, taking advantage of this path up the steep willow bluff. The tussocks are cratered, signs of the animals feeding. Finally I stop on a hilltop. To the north fifty caribou graze. To the west hundreds stretch in a line, coming my way. A lone bull, with antlers still, watches me from a quarter mile off. Mountains stand misty in faintly falling snow. A portion of my mind flashes to *caribou tongue!* and *brisket soup!* Mentally I frame a photo. But I leave my rifle in its scabbard, my camera in its bag, and only inhale cold air and companionship.

The oncoming herd is led by a bull, a surprise. But he's at the end of rut; maybe he's still confused. In caribou world, females lead. Something we might learn from these creatures. Thin ice, bad weather, hunters waiting— it's almost always a cow that leads the herd, often with a calf on her heels. Bulls hang to the back, more concerned with polishing their antlers.

Lately, word from up the Kobuk River has been of a lean fall, no caribou on the tundra. This past season has been a strange one: the herds delayed migrating from the north until after Freezeup in late October. Some folks believe this is because of climate changes, warmer and later falls; some accuse the invasion of sport hunters from the lower forty-eight states.

Traditionally, caribou come through the region in autumn heading south to their wintering grounds. They are such a part of this place, practically seasons on the land, flowing across the tundra. Every year we hope there are enough for meat and for the company of sorts that they provide. And with the herds come nonlocal wolves and wolverines, and rowdy ravens who don't know the home rules (what is allowed to be borrowed and what draws a bullet). One fall the river ran thin ice for weeks, and thousands of caribou plodded east along the north

Previous pages:
Pausing to check
the ice

shore, day and night coming through the yard. My dog team lost a lot of sleep. I burned through the calories, hoofing the tundra carrying my brother's camera. Another spring there were no caribou through most of April, then one day the far bank of the river was lined as if the Confederate army were coming. Animals poured out of the willows on the far shore and filled the river ice.

Now, on the hilltop, the herd forks into three streams flowing slowly east to cross at the mouth of the Noatak River and plod around the distant shore of Kobuk Lake. I turn the other direction and travel northwest on rough tussocks, into low hills, hoping to say hello to another creature. If caribou are old companions, this species feels like a new friend.

147
hanging with the
hang-out kings

Mountains serrate the northern horizon, rising to Mount Noak, tapering away again into expanse and sky. In these hills and on up the Chukchi coast to Rabbit Creek, Red Dog, and beyond, a recently returned prehistoric animal roams, one I didn't grow up with but have grown to love here on the windswept coast.

Miles in the distance, I spot the telltale black mounds, a band of fifteen or twenty muskoxen. Unlike caribou or bears—or even moose—these animals are not inclined to try to escape. They are family, and this windswept range is their home. They have no wish to run.

As I motor over a ridge, the shaggy animals rise. They appear huge and foreboding, built in the head and shoulders like buffalo. Still a mile away, I park and put together my camera, taking my time and staying skylined. I don't stalk them. These muskoxen, I've found, will accept my presence. I eye the sky mistrustfully. Along this Arctic coast wind can rise quickly and leave hunters lost in a blizzard yards from their sleds. Now, far to the south out over the sea ice, the blue overhead fades into neon orange. Sun leaks through a strip of cloud and the land glows in shades of lavender.

On crisp snow I walk closer. The black mounds turn and face me in a line. They are hoofed and hung with thick draping hair, helmeted with curved and deadly horns. If I didn't know better I'd run. These animals would like that best: when a predator runs, they don't have to.

Following pages:
Caribou crossing
frozen ponds; Jade
Mountains in the
background

In their eyes is the soft and thoughtful look of a million years on the planet. Like the caribou, they have something we could learn; muskoxen's secret to survival is simply to not waste energy. This is an animal whose ancestors walked the Pleistocene beside our own, foraging the steppelike tundra and stony hilltops. Their bones lie in human campsites from Ice Age days and before, spread from the Desna River north of the Black Sea to the Russian Plain, Greenland, and our backyard—Alaska. Their history

Adult bull muskoxen after a winter storm

is carved in rock alongside human history in Paleolithic cave drawings in Roc de Sers, France, and other locations. I know these details not from being a caveman or from my experience shivering in the herds' midst, waiting days for a photograph, but from a book, *Muskoxen and their Hunters,* by Peter Lent. My dad's old friend, it turns out, continued on as a biologist, while his assistant was seduced away by the tundra, Eskimos, and the animals they had studied.

Umiŋmaich—muskoxen—disappeared from this region before my grandparents were born. They were extirpated from all of Alaska in the late 1800s. Whalers, Native hunters, and white explorers, all with firearms, marked their demise. Populations in Canada and Greenland also shrank with the advancement of technology.

Around the time that kid named Nelson Greist and his family were migrating from Barrow south, the Alaska territorial government arranged to have a few dozen muskoxen captured in Greenland and shipped by steamer to New York. The poor animals were quarantined in New Jersey, shipped west by train to Seattle, sent once more on steamer to Seward, by rail to Fairbanks—and finally let out of their original crates half a year after being captured.

Caribou would have died. The muskoxen arrived fat and healthy, attesting to that secret of their species' survival through harsh and varied eons past: their ability to hang out.

When I was five years old, in 1970, the Alaska Department of Fish and Game released thirty-six muskoxen at Cape Thompson, and the same number on the Seward Peninsula. Of course my family knew nothing about this; we didn't see one along the river for a couple of decades. Later, thirty-four more animals were released on Cape Thompson, and an additional thirty-five were transported to the Seward Peninsula. Others had already been sent to the Arctic National Wildlife Refuge; some remained in Fairbanks, Nunivak Island, and other locations. But every last one in Alaska stems from the original gene pool of those transplanted Greenlandic animals. Every muskox in the state could hail every other muskox as "bro," or "cuz."

Muskoxen in
ground blizzard

During the recent Ice Age and the end of the Pleistocene, dramatic biotic transformation swept the land and swept it again. Herbivores that roamed here—huge woolly mammoths, mastodons, steppe bison, western camels, miniature wild horses—vanished from the earth. Saber-toothed tigers, steppe lions, scimitar cats faded into oblivion. Through it all, muskoxen survived. Until the latecomers, humans, the predator of predators, arrived.

These days, muskoxen are back. Lone bulls have spread far: across the Seward Peninsula, up the Kobuk, and east to the far-flung headwaters of the Noatak. Humans are again hunting them, and brown bears too are relearning how to kill this strange "new" creature. And I hope the muskox will survive this, too. It would be sad, I think, and not a good sign if this species were to go extinct.

I tamp in my tripod, compose a photo. A bitter north wind is rising. I stand and wait, for a change in the herd. My thoughts wander, thinking about these animals and how they made it to the present. Somewhere along the way, muskoxen developed their unique survival style. They don't waste. Muskoxen keep it simple. They don't migrate. They don't crater down through snow for food. They work together, protecting family units using their protective circle. They are peaceful and won't charge unless they're provoked. They make fat during the Arctic summer, a lot of fat. And they grow thick pelts with hair twenty inches long that hangs like a skirt down around their short legs—more hair and a warmer coat than any other animal, insulated with qiviut, a downy wool softer than cashmere. Muskoxen have four stomachs, to wring every last nutrient out of the low-quality vegetation they eat. They stay sedentary and keep their metabolism extremely low, instead of running for a living the way caribou must do.

They stay in the group, form the circle, horns out; when the show is over, the brown bear gone, the wolves retreated, muskoxen lay back down and go to sleep and let the blizzards blow over them.

With short legs and nowhere on the planet to run, they live danger-ously close to the environmental margin. Muskoxen live on that line, that thin good-bye edge of extinction. Theirs is a simple, efficient, very different-from-human approach to a parallel journey through time. If they can't hang out and take it easy, they can't survive. And who can say, *umiŋmaich* may outlive us all.

I go now, collapse my tripod, turn and leave these animals their peace and privacy. I walk the mile back toward my machine.

Previous pages:
Muskoxen in the
Igichuk Hills

The wolf is on the river ice long enough for half a cup of coffee to cool. Long enough for me to forget again that wilderness is being chased away from this place. It's twenty-nine below and I step into my sod house to grab a jacket, put the mug on the barrel stove, and shut its draft for safety. I'm back out in time to see an Anchorage Native politician on a Japanese snowmobile shoot the wolf.

There are two snowmobiles out there suddenly, and one dead wolf, all black and white on the snow. Joyous whoops float across to me; the sound arrives faint and is swallowed into the cold expanse. The men drag the hundred-pound animal to a sled. In the distance they pause to piss and point, then roar down the far shore, searching for tracks to lead them to the rest of the pack. All things that I have done before. But now I stumble inside and sit on the kindling stump by the stove.

There's a war going on up here on the last frontier. It has the elements of those Middle East wars on the nightly news: there's crude oil, of course, and hundreds of millions of dollars are coming here from somewhere else, propaganda enshrouds all, and we carry guns, too. The difference is that our guns are aimed at animals and we humans are fighting over who gets to pull the triggers. In the Alaskan bush, the battle cry is "Subsistence!" Sadly, that has also been the major casualty.

Subsistence—Alaska's conundrum—arose as more than just another word in the white man's dictionary in the 1970s in the time of the Alaska Native Claims Settlement Act (ANCSA). This act and the settlement of land issues were necessary to begin the parceling and surveying and dividing of Alaska, to clear the trail for the Trans-Alaska Pipeline and other oil and mineral extraction. *Subsistence* was a term chosen by the drafters of ANCSA to describe living off the land. Not living off the land mining, working at Prudhoe Bay, or guiding big game hunters, but living with minimal cash, gathering meat and fish and berries, wearing skins and furs.

With ANCSA, the federal government granted Alaska Natives a portion of the land (which was already theirs), plus half a billion dollars and property-tax-free status. It required that they conduct themselves as corporations, each Native person a shareholder. Overnight, the trail from hunting and gathering to capitalism was widened and paved. And every last person—some running, some dragging their feet, even some misplaced barefoot white boys—ended up on that trail.

The government then began saturating rural Native communities with more money, hundreds and hundreds of thousands of dollars per person, in an attempt to bring living conditions closer to national norms. (National norms apparently don't include storing fermented walrus flipper in the ground or using a kerosene can for a crapper— in other words, living with what you have: subsisting.) The excess in money brought with it excesses in alcoholism, suicide, drug abuse, and corresponding off-the-chart statistics that made available even more grants and government funding. Hence, today, we are awash in dollars, those little green soldiers of capitalism.

Some suggest that ANCSA and all the resulting cash were part of a calculated plan to draw Alaska Natives into the system, and by dividing Alaska and deeding land ownership to thirteen Native groups, the treaty made development not just possible but, in the end, necessary.

Conspiracy or corporate-world reality, this part of the Arctic that so recently was simply the land, a seemingly endless expanse of rich and sustaining nature with sparsely scattered villages and families living off it, is now the NANA Region. The Northwest Alaska Native Association is a corporation and must survive as one. NANA now has in its mission statement "to be a multi-billion dollar company," and already celebrating twenty years in operation is its pride, the Red Dog Mine. Between the villages of Kivalina and Noatak, NANA and the Canadian mining conglomerate Teck Cominco have built the largest lead and zinc strip mine in the world. NANA has other plans for the land, including a gold, silver, and copper mine in the drainages of rivers that flow into the upper Kobuk. While this might create hundreds of jobs, none of it engenders hope for the land remaining as it was, or for people living "subsistence."

In 1980 a second act was passed, setting Alaska up for the present urban—versus—rural hostilities. The Alaska National Interest Land Claims Act (ANILCA) in one swoop established more national park lands than all those in the lower forty-eight states combined and promised "rural preference" for subsistence hunting and fishing on those federal lands. This became law, although few noticed at the time, especially those living closest to what remained of a subsistence lifestyle.

Under ANILCA's decree, the state of Alaska managed fish and game on the recently parceled state, federal, and Native lands. This worked for a decade, until an Anchorage man named McDowell filed suit, claiming that the Alaska Constitution guaranteed equal access to hunting and fishing for all Alaskans. The state was trapped between its own constitution and federal mandate.

The federal government stepped in to keep its promise. A quick constitutional amendment was anticipated to bring the state in line with ANILCA, but year after year urban legislators blocked a referendum from the ballot. Native groups accused the state of bowing to sport-hunting groups, supporting cultural genocide, and even endorsing starvation. They filed suit demanding sovereignty in the form of Indian Country status—the right to make and enforce their own laws. When the U.S. Supreme Court ruled against them, they swung their support behind federal management.

Further suits have been filed over navigable waterways that were state controlled, then later ruled to be under federal jurisdiction; urban sportsmen's groups charged that a constitutional amendment would make them second-class citizens; proponents of states' rights sued. Supporters of secession from the Union even entered the fray. The parade of court decisions and appeals has left the lines of authority transient and unclear to all involved. In this way, urban and rural Alaskans have turned against each other in a bitter range war. Meanwhile, discussion of the fact that true subsistence has been overrun by technology and the idea that trophy hunting in the twenty-first century is perverted is, of course, off-limits.

This war is big-fisted and confusing, the truth is taboo, and friends on both sides will hate me for writing about it. People won't see my love of providing, of hunting. They won't see that I criticize not subsistence but what has infiltrated it. They won't hear that I'm only saying we need to be more respectful or we will lose the last of this way of life. I could be quiet and kill wolves instead, out in the solace of frostbite and wind. I'd be richer and more respected. Maybe happier. But I'd have to live with someone not myself.

Today, after watching the wolf die, I can't stay in the confines of my snowshoe trails between the outhouse, igloo, and cache. I pack a stove, wall tent, sleeping bag, caribou sleeping hides, and a grub box on my sled. This hickory sled was made by my father, but the lashings are nylon, no longer babiche strips cut from caribou neck hide. The sleeping bag, sewn by my mother, is insulated with duck, crane, swan, and goose down. I fashioned the stove and pipe from five-gallon Chevron kerosene cans. It's thirty-one below and I drive a snowgo, an Arctic Cat Bearcat 440. It requires gas and new parts, neither native species in this place. Tied on the back are the birch snowshoes Oliver Cameron built for my brother thirty-five years ago and nine thousand dollars worth of Nikon camera and lenses; lashed to the cowling is an *ugruk* skin scabbard, in it an AR-15 rifle.

As always I ruminate, questioning how much I gather from nature and recycle from scrap, and how much I've become some strange yuppie, one who happens to enjoy whale *muktuk* and frostbite.

Alvin hunting
wolves on the
spring tundra

Across the river ice stretches the drifted south bank, and then willows and thick spruce, and finally open tundra. There in a circle of snowgo tracks, I find a week-old naked wolf carcass. The Arctic Cat tracks I recognize as belonging to Alvin, more and more these years an expert wolf hunter. Raven crap blotches the skull and stomach. The wolf is as large as a young caribou. I think about chopping off a hind leg, for dinner, but I hurry away.

The tundra is windswept and rough with the exposed grassy heads of tussocks. Lone stunted spruce hunker miles in the distance like bachelor trolls. The snow glows in all the pastel blues of Arctic day, and on the horizon against the lower faces of the mountains timber drapes in black beards. The cold is complete. As far as I've come and as far as I can see, not one living thing moves, and I wonder about the hunger of those people of the past.

In the dense spruce guarding the flanks of the Kobuk Sand Dunes, the snow is deep and the terrain steep. My snowgo tips over, mired and pinned against a tree. Silence rings among the laden branches, and I am almost relieved to lace on my snowshoes and break trail for this machine. A wolverine passed this way before the last snow, and a squirrel has been out, maybe last week. The edges of its tracks are crumbled, sublimated. A marten followed, last night or this morning, tracking the squirrel. The snow in its prints is set, but not as firm as it will be.

I hear a whimpering in the trees. My hand twitches for a rifle, but I go on, leaning and peering forward. Silence lives here in these trees. But what else? Finally there comes a breath of sound and I am not certain if it is real or imagined. Tucked up in the branches, a porcupine clings. It is cold for him to be out of his den. We peer at each other, both with frost around our eyes and puffs of breath dissipating. I consider shaking him down for dinner but decline. Winter porcupine tastes like a spruce slab, and besides, it is nice to have him here.

Before dark I pitch my tent along the creek on the west end of the dunes. Ptarmigan feed there in the willows and I shoot one, and boil it with ramen and eat it with a Ziploc bag of *muktuk* that Chuck

Schaeffer gave me in Kotzebue. It is beluga *muktuk*, raw and soaked in Tabasco sauce, not boiled and plain, the way I learned to eat it. My chewing is loud and I stop often to listen for the howl of wolves. Why I'm here is not exactly clear.

Hunting is installed in my heart, as sacred as eating and breathing. It is a very separate thing from some Outsider's paper regulations. I'm not alone in this conviction. Here on the old frontier the approaching modern mesh of law feels like a gill net set to drown our souls. But the truth? We're already hooked. We have swallowed technology and are wriggling to avoid the shackles that make it work: rules and laws.

Our need for foods and furs from the land has shrunk exponentially as the Gore-Tex and plastic, Pepsi and Banquet chicken have come off the airplanes. But our ability to harvest animals grows with every Ski-Doo and Ruger rifle. In the villages now a new generation has been raised in HUD houses, on basketball, satellite TV, and Nintendo; salted in the same barrel with a tidal wave of government grants, Canadian whiskey, and longing for tangible tradition. Out of the turmoil of change, hunting has held its venerated position. As the old ways fade, hunting absorbs their meanings. Doctor, lawyer, president—there is still no higher status than hunter.

Unfortunately, hunting itself has altered. *Subsistence*, the word, now at times includes everything from bringing *aana*—grandma—bags of geese to video-game-like herd-shooting of caribou with assault rifles from hundred-mile-an-hour snowmobiles.

"He always catch"—half a century ago the difference between life and starvation—is still our region's highest compliment. But lost along the trail to today are the bulk of the ancestral requisites of hunger-driven hunting, often including tracking the wounded, tanning hides, reverence for the dead. The elders acknowledge this, shake their heads, and have little idea what to do about it.

We are living through big change, hard times in a new way. We still eat a lot of meat, fish, and berries. The dying of subsistence as a *lifestyle* doesn't negate the importance of wild food from the land, for many of us essential to feeling and being alive. The gathering of wild food has changed but still provides nourishment to our spirits too, something that doesn't seem to be coming off those airplanes.

In Anchorage this subsistence battle may be about a change in regulations; here it is not so simple. Here hunting and fishing laws have long been moot. Boundaries have been boundaries of the spirit and of one's own strengths, abilities, and needs—a "freedom" long gone from the contiguous states. In subsistence country the battle has two fronts: one against Outside trophy hunters coming to take animals, and the other against any regulation at all. We are living in the twilight of the frontier, in the headlights of America. What we're doing about this transition is pretending to be in the past.

Tonight in pinching cold that I can taste, alone in vast silence, I am thinking that here, as in the Old West, it is what we've lost that marks who we are much more than these things we've gained. I'm sad, aware that in my short years, gathering off the land as the mainstay of a lifestyle has all but gone extinct. Gone with it are much of its logic, lessons, and values.

In the morning my campstove is out and icy. My sleeping bag and wolf ruff are sticky with dots of pitch. I'm annoyed with myself for hurrying last night, for cutting a green ridgepole instead of searching for a dead one for my canvas tent. The pitch stains will join those "rabbit tracks" along the wall, where Alvin's Coke cans exploded years ago.

The sun is about to clear the dunes. I snowshoe upcreek a few miles, dodging steaming overflow and listening to redpolls flit in the alders. This is early March and the sun is yellow now and shares a little warmth against the cold. Otter slides crisscross the creek. I finger my .22 pistol. For a few years I've been thinking about sewing a pair of otter overpants. They'd be silent for hunting, and warm. I've shot otters, and trapped them, too. This hat on my head is otter, sewn by Clara Williams. But the question hangs, do I really *need* otter pants? Nylon is okay and here to stay. At the Native store in Ambler sixty dollars buys

Seth heading out on snowshoes to check traps (Photo by Stacey Glaser)

me Walls Insulated Bib Overalls. And otters are tough for me to kill—they play, sliding off knolls and down buried beaver lodges, stopping to nuzzle each other like sweethearts.

Back at the tent, I build a fire on the ice and cook oatmeal in last night's ptarmigan pot. Afterward, I snowgo along the dunes, following a maze of wolf tracks west into the deep snow of an old burn. The light is good and I daydream that I'll finally get that photo of a wolf pack downing a moose, an image portraying true nature, whatever that might be. But photography is not hunting. My eyes aren't the predators that once pried apart every twig on the land. Hunting was once the thread in every stitch of my life, before technology and dollars unraveled me to a point where I could not eat, wear, or justify all I could hunt.

In the afternoon I loop east. A few miles from my campsite, on the wide open white of the dunes, I cross fresh wolf tracks. Ten wolves heading straight for my tent! I follow and hit snowgo tracks, one machine with no sled, going and returning, on top of the wolf tracks. The wolf trails fan out. The snow is soft and leg holes stretch out into a run—animals hunted.

In a lonesome amphitheater in the center of the dunes I come across a figure eight where the machine passed a wolf, both trails folded back, and the wolf tumbled.

The air is still, and quiet. There's blood flung on the snow, Sorel boot tracks and an empty red Federal ammo carton. The snowgo track returns east from where it came. Why, I wonder? Who here stops at one wolf? Men now spend hundreds, even thousands of dollars more to shoot furbearers than their wives—who do the sewing—spend to order tanned skins from H. E. Goldberg and other fur suppliers. Dead animals equal prestige and are symbols of a good provider—a splinter of the past still intact. Getting the whole pack is the way to have your name sweep villages hundreds of miles away.

And the wolf's trail? Going backward, his path might meander hundreds of miles, finally fading under the last snowfall, but it ends right here on the dunes.

I break camp, weary with the company of the only fool around, and aware that the word of nine wolves will be out.

At home at the igloo, I build a fire in the barrel stove and head down to the river in the twilight to chip open my water hole. Thoughts tower in the all-embracing silence. Packing buckets back up the bluff, I notice footprints in the snow where someone has stolen gasoline from my cache and flung my orange jug behind a tree. I now see why the hunter abandoned the rest of the wolf pack. I am still a good enough tracker to recognize the aggressive lugs—the same powerful Polaris snowmobile as on the dunes—and find a few blood crystals and a Pepsi can heeled into a drift.

Late in the spring evening's blue dusk, I tune in KOTZ in Kotzebue, hoping simply for a song here in the silence. Instead I catch a recording of a person testifying to a Senate committee on, of course, subsistence.

I feel twisted by politics, tired of wishing us humans to be better, to be more respectful of animals. "Real subsistence?" I demand of the sod walls: "Who? Where? All who don't drive Hondas and Arctic Cats and airplanes, who don't eat chicken more often than muskrat—you six go ahead, take it all, please!" I pace the old floor, longing to respect someone the way my dad respected Mabel Thomas all those years ago. Longing to stomp down this net of looming regulations, to believe in and fight for a lifestyle, one with accurate descriptions and honesty and *wild food from the land*.

Pages of my scribblings lie on the boards leaking hope and questions. *Are Ziplocs subsistence? . . . The biggest threat to living off the land is people flying around and driving around shooting things that are living off the land. . . . No one adds up the sheer poundage of fallen animals. . . . Freezers have become staging areas for the dump. . . . Are we really stupid enough to be arguing over whose ancestors were more deserving?*

The Iñupiat have a word, *suakataq*, that is one of my favorites. An elder can get on the CB and *suakataq* a whole village for not helping a stranger, for drinking too much, or for arguing over ice-fishing spots. I find myself wanting to *suakataq* all involved: starting with some bad behavior in the name of something as virtuous as gathering food. I would *suakataq* out of disappointment for the huge discrepancy between rhetoric and reality, and out of fear of what we might lose here.

Trophy hunting is a harder subject to imagine how to *suakataq* because I have no understanding for shooting an animal for sport. Only questions: You who fly so far to kill Alaskan animals, where do you call home and what do you care about? Alaska gives away money, most years more than a thousand dollars to every man, woman, and child. Economically speaking, we need Belgian businessmen and Illinois orthodontists coming up to shoot big moose the way Africa needs more dead elephants.

But I'm no elder, and my voice can never be the voice of the People. I understand this weariness with white intervention. Still, it leaves me tormented, to be from out on this land, devoted to this land, and silent. And it leaves me asking, What kind of life is that, and what kind of creature lives so selfishly?

Outside, the spring expands into sunny nights. The caribou migrate north. The herd is as large as ever recorded, 500,000 animals. As a result, there is no shortage of wolverines, wolves, and bears. The land's cyclical plentitude has coincided with technology's rapid rise, making fools out of those of us who attempt to warn of its potential for devastation. Thousands upon thousands of caribou fill the river ice, packing the snow with trails. Herds sweep through, and halt, bivouacked armies. Caribou stand behind every knoll, in every draw, lie on every pond like Rwandan refugees. The sun melts out cutbanks, and the first juncos arrive, and then white-crowned sparrows and myrtle warblers. Nights are bright, the land glowing. Travel is finer than in any other season. And meanwhile—somewhere, everywhere—development spreads its metal root hairs across Alaska, stretching three thousand miles from Attu to Ketchikan, a thousand from Homer to Barrow. Now the Park Service wants tourists, the state wants roads, the Native corporations lust for profit, everyone needs a job. This wilderness of ours has glass walls. Too many eyes and too many dollars are watching this place.

And still the land shines under a rejuvenated sun. It is hard not to burst into a smile. It's Breakup here along this big river. Spring. The water coming up fast. Fat tasty pintails skim overhead. Any day now there will be fresh seagull eggs. Ice pans turn down the current, bumping against willows with blossoms fanned out at their tops. The water is still rising. Rising faster than we remember.

Following pages:
Caribou filling
the river on their
migration north

bob and carrie come out of the hills

Bob and Carrie in their apartment in Kotzebue, 2005

"We rode a huge airplane, about the biggest anyone has ever seen," Bob Uhl tells me. "I guess it was a 747, but probably twice as long. Man, there was a lot of people on there."

Carrie limps around scowling, rubbing her knee. "*Arii*, that airport's too big. If Johnson Greene never helped us—. We were so thankful for him." She grimaces. Bob describes what might have been an alien city: the Anchorage airport.

Bob and Carrie went to Anchorage last month. Before it happened, I heard about the proposed journey all around Kotzebue. "Go Anchorage" people say here, and in this case it wasn't gossip, it was news.

I stopped in at the apartment where they now spend midwinters, at the Senior Center housing. The place is bright and well lit, warm from no apparent source. Water comes out of a tap and leaves by itself. These are strange and disquieting events to these "camp" people.

Until recently Bob and Carrie always lived across Kotzebue Sound at Sisualik. There they have grown to be icons of the region, along with Lena Jones over in Jones Camp, old man John Schaeffer along the north side of Kobuk Lake, Louie and Lulu Nelson at Ivik, and surely others I'm forgetting. But a couple of winters ago, old age and new weather patterns aligned to drive the Uhls to town.

Thin ice late into fall, overflow on the trail, and bad storms had all kept the couple from making their fall migration off the coast to the protection of their winter cabin up in the trees. Pinned down on the windblown shore, Bob had frozen his hands trying to get a few yards from the door out to feed his dogs. No one could cross the ice because of the overflow; planes couldn't fly in the blizzard. With his hands in bad shape, and still shrouded in whiteout conditions and running low on firewood, Bob worried what might happen to Carrie if an accident befell him. With over half a century on that side of the sound, their lives are entwined with nature; it was an agonizing decision to move to town. And because of where they would be staying, Bob found it necessary to shoot his dogs.

In town it followed that he developed chest pain—who wouldn't upon leaving the land and daily companions for a nearly windowless apartment in Kotzebue?—and he got snared in modern medicine. Eventually he was told by doctors that he had to "go Anchorage." For tests.

173
bob and carrie
come out of
the hills

At their apartment that day there was unusual tension around the table. Bob finally explained that their granddaughter, Kathleen Sherman, was arranging Alaska Airlines tickets for them. She was also trying to come up with an ID for Bob. He had a driver's license, in good shape; the only problem was that it had expired in 1971.

Bob settled down and served me *quaq* whitefish, seal oil, roasted caribou ribs, crackers, and salmonberries. He seemed his usual self: twinkling eyes, full of knowledge about fish, flowers, and furbearers. And he was equally positive, enthusiastic, even curious now about X-rays and this procedure they had in mind for him. "A *cat* scam?" he said.

I sat eating, worrying about these two naive friends. Finally in possession of superior knowledge on at least one subject, I blurted warnings about the Transportation Security Administration rules and the

Anchorage airport. It all sounded like Nazi Germany. Bob suggested I try the *muktuk*.

Identification? No, he'd never had a problem identifying himself. And local people had informed him and Carrie that Anchorage had places to get licenses. Wasn't Anchorage the capital of licensing this and that and whatever?

I wasn't making headway, arguing my ID bunk with two of the most renowned people in the northwest Arctic. "You can't just buy an ID there," I said. "You could get stuck in Anchorage."

Bob looked at his thawing fish.

Carrie clicked off KOTZ radio. "Bob! You aren't doing nothing! Call Kathleen!"

Carrie, a full-blooded Iñupiaq elder, is practically a globe-trotter in comparison to her Californian husband. She's flown to the villages, and been to Anchorage a handful of times, to Musicale, and to visit her brother and other relatives living down in the city. Bob is forthcoming yet vague about his experiences below the Arctic Circle. You have to listen closely. ("My mother and stepdad came up a few years back. When was that, Carrie? Before snowgos, wasn't it?") Some time in the 1950s, it turns out. I've pried and found out, sure, since he moved here Bob has traveled to southern cities—a single trip to Fairbanks, thirty years ago.

I walked out their door deeply concerned, that the distant doctors and hospitals might swallow them up, that I might have to charter a Cessna to fly these "unidentifiable" elders home. Passing through the Senior Center, I ran into another old family friend, Tommy Douglas, slumped in a wheelchair. He was old and had had a stroke since I last saw him. I stopped to say hi, pretty sure he didn't recognize this white guy. "Alwus carry spare clothes," he said, deadly serious. "If you go through ice, you hafta make fire." His lips were huge and one side of his face hung. "You gonna freeze if you never carry dry clothes. Matches, too."

A week later I'm back at the Uhls' table, hearing about monster jets, and about Carrie hurting her knee trying to get down the aisle, and about Bob's experience with the CAT scam. Always wanting to know the past, I attempt to steer the conversation around to his impression of Anchorage, now versus 1948.

Bob pauses. "Well. Back then there weren't very many autoMO-biles," he says.

He'd been stationed at Fort Richardson but lived at Fishcamp, the First Combat Intelligence Platoon, part of Castner's Cutthroats. Bob's duties had included caring for 250 U.S. Army sled dogs. That job as a dog team soldier was what brought him north to Kotzebue. It happened that he met Carrie and headed into the hills instead of returning to his family in California. Ever.

"*Arii*, we don't want to hear again about your Cutthroat," Carrie chides him. Her knee hurts. She's pacing, beside herself to be home and have her husband home. "When Bob has to go back, next month, you'll take him," she tells me.

"You weren't bothered with mechanical vehicles of any sort at all out there." Bob is still talking, about Fort Richardson again, 1948. "It was like any fish camp.

"This trip was right through the middle of all the mechanized revolution. It was very hard to see the geography of Anchorage, the lakes and rabbit tracks and such."

He pauses to reflect. "The good part about it was a lot of people were really helpful. Same people as there were years ago—friendly and helpful, if they got to know you were in need of help."

Naturalist, hunter, observer: Bob is a philosopher like no one else I know. He loves to mull things over; it about drives Carrie crazy. I catch him grinning. He dips his tea bag in and out of his cup. "A person has to decide," he muses, "whether it would just be easier to go ahead and die or go back to that place."

175

bob and carrie
come out of
the hills

Following pages:
Autumn on the
tundra

"Shhh . . . we're lookin' for gobies!" I attempt to hush my twenty-two-month-old daughter, China, as we hike up the path from our sod house. Around us birch leaves are beginning to spatter the ground with the yellow paint of fall. Spruce and alder branches snag our hair. Across the distances come the caws of ravens counting coup over animals down. The loudest sounds are the gnarled knuckles of trail roots grabbing at my shoes. *Gobi* is China's word for caribou. I have no problem incorporating her locution.

On a stretch less steep I let her walk. She points out trees, spruce cones, poplar leaves. We've recently spent the summer in Kotzebue, where these things are not. "Moose tracks!" she says excitedly. Just now I'd had too much on my mind to notice. Important adult concerns, ones that seem never to cease multiplying. We hunch down and grin at each other: her thrilled, me impressed. With her vocabulary of fifty or a hundred words, this latest comment of hers is a large and clear chunk of information. And she hasn't seen anything moose in the most recent quarter of her lifetime. How does she remember all this stuff? I need to figure that out. One thing I have figured out is that this kid didn't inherit this dyslexic half-built brain of mine.

We continue along the trail. It's a game and family path, padded down over the decades by my parents' boots and Kole's and my bare feet. Caribou hairs in an alder fork and then blond grizzly hairs up a scarred pitchy spruce, and China's moose sign, all remind me of a childhood

China Kantner
(eleven months old)
picking blueberries,
1998

cognizance I've forgotten: regardless of the proximity to my birthplace down the ridge, my tracks have always been the rarest ones here.

China stuffs her tiny hands with cones and we stop repeatedly while she presents me special ones. She's humming some account of this journey, or an anthology of others. I glance ahead, fidgety, trying not to grab her up and rush on.

I need to get to the top, out onto the tundra, while the light is long, for pictures. I guess I need to. I mock myself with a well-worn question: What is a photographic slide besides a leftover image, a plastic and transparent one at that? Paying attention to China and to the land's daily news, if not a career, is certainly more genuine. I pace up the trail, longing as I do so often for a need as pure as food, to teach me again how to hear the land's voices the way I heard them when the hunting life permeated my days. To China my rushing is senseless, baffling. Hurrying hasn't developed in her brain, though it will if she hangs around her dad. It will.

The trees thin. We step out onto the sprawl of trail-veined tundra alight with the dying glory of fall. I point ahead, to snap her attention off the blueberries. "Jade Mountains," she informs me in her brand-new miniature voice. All mountains, even low hills, are the Jade Mountains to her, although in this case she's correct. A group of caribou graze in the distance, cows and calves, no bulls. The sun is already high, the light washed out, contrasty and bright. No stunning photos await me here. "Jade Mountains," I agree, no longer murmuring. Time and peace lie around us, plenty to think about, and what I'm thinking is this: Africa, Australia, America, every continent and every country I've ever visited—somehow my eyes compared all mountains to the Jades. It makes me proud that they will always be China's first mountains, too.

From away south, across the tundra on the far side of the river, floats the drone of an airplane. "Annie! Annie!" China peers between dwarf spruce, her height, though they are probably ten times her age. Andy Koster, a friend whom China has a crush on, flies a mail plane for Bering Air. I try to explain to her that as capable and great-looking a guy as he is, and even with that British accent, he doesn't fly every airplane in the sky. She ignores me and studies the tundra for berries. I don't spot the plane but get a fairly clear view of how the teenage years could go.

Back down at the house, she has no interest in going inside. It's a quiet day along the river, calm, sunny, and unseasonable for September. The meat is in. Most of the friends who might once have boated down to visit have moved closer to towns, cities, and sun. Nothing really has to get done this afternoon, but I'm a little too far from a greenhorn to forget that tomorrow could carpet the ground with snow, for a couple

China and Seth sharpening the chainsaw (Photo by Stacey Glaser)

hundred days. My mind runs down an impatient list that ends with that chronic bush chore, working on the chainsaw.

China struggles to find words to explain to me the awesome trip from Kotzebue, the boat, gobies, and *mo lalu*. *Mo lalu*, of course, means water. Being a parent, I wonder who would ever say *water* when they could mouth the musical *mo lalu*. China adores being outside. This came as a great relief to me, I who *live* outside. When our child was on the way, I suffered great trepidation. *What if she's an inside kid?* Later, I accidentally froze her cheeks skiing when she was six months old; at eighteen months she snowgoed with us more than a hundred miles up here from Kotzebue. The next day I took her down to the river to open a water hole. The ice was slippery with chips and when I turned my back she slipped, one arm up like a little bundled Statue of Liberty, headfirst in the water hole. And I wonder, did all that immersion help?

Now not yet two, she sits on a log, wrenches her tiny green rubber boots off, and heads down the hill. She's undeterred by countless rose thorns in her feet, utterly familiar with the words, *mosquito bite*. Across miles of distance and time my childhood leaks back in the prick of those thorns and bites. I recognize the faint reflection of a barefoot boy born and raised on this same bluff. Suddenly how thankful I am that this beautiful blond bundle came along, with her unpolluted perspective and free-scattering of appreciation for the chickadees and stinkbugs that cross the path of her days.

We move down the trail toward my parents' old igloo. She points out cranberries and bends, panting from the constriction of diaper and belly, reaching tiny sausage fingers. Her lips pucker at the sourness of the berries.

"We need to go work on Howie's cache," I suggest, not optimistic.

"Howie's cache," she says and blurts on, desperate to impart information, "and, and the old ligaloo!"

Actually, I've given up on this older igloo, I explain, given it to the animals who want in. What I'm trying now is to tear down my mom's old cache, salvage the tin roofing for my dad's. There's nothing valuable in there—caribou leggings, leaky rain gear, spare parts for engines long dead—though ravens have been poking in to investigate. Somehow I've convinced myself, as usual, that it needs to be done, now.

Maybe it does, maybe it doesn't. China feels equally strongly about these berries. She's a project, too, the finest, most exhausting, rewarding, risky work of art. It's been slowly dawning on me that this kid is an altogether different effort from the rest of my life. She is joy that stretches from the past through this moment and into the future. Most of what else I do is merely the present. Now it makes sense to me, the way sow bears protect their cubs.

We sit and pluck dark plump cranberries. Just when I think China's mind is entirely on eating them, she points at two animal pellets in the leaves, wide-eyed and excited again. "Bocabine toods!"

city boy

Writer's notes to self:

Today at thirty below with west wind at thirty I rode China to kindergarten in the bicycle buggy. With a box cutter, cut a square of caribou hide for her to sit on. The razor broke in the cold, my ears froze, fingers too. The bike free-wheeled; the rear axle wouldn't grab when I pedaled. I heated it with a blowtorch—after I got the blowtorch warm enough to burn. On the way to school China's little voice informed me that her face was frozen. I stopped, melted it, the bike stopped working. We made it, though my ear still might be a different story.

Afternoon, I biked over to Greg Garrett's. I'm house sitting. Lots of sliding on ice and falls on the way. His oil stove, a Monitor heater, had quit. I pressed the orange button, started it, rode on to Susan Bucknell's (where I'm also house sitting). Her lock was frozen. Thought I had the wrong key. Thawed it, freezing fingers. The door finally opened. Heater going, bathtub drain frozen.

    Went back to Greg's. The toilet had frozen; the heater was working. I rode to the rec center to warm up in the sauna. The power went out. Bundled back up and went home: China was throwing up (special Kotzebue flu). I couldn't keep up with the vomit. Stacey called from Greg's: "Seth! The Monitor is flashing 'burner status'?"

Arranged to have a neighbor, Ruth, drive Stacey's work truck to the college in the morning and at same time asked Ruth if she might have some spare stove oil.

"Maybe some old dirty stuff."

Tried to ride to Greg's. Bike wouldn't work; pounded on rear axle with hammer. Thirty-six below, windy, three hours at Greg's, outside in the dark climbing up on tall tank, pouring hot water on oil filter, stove-oil soaked gloves. Inside, all faucets running, all lights, all kitchen burners, oven door open. Temp creeping up though no luck with Monitor.

Rode to Susan's, lock frozen, heater fine, bike quit. Back to Greg's, repeat of earlier, finally got heater running, headed home.

Stacey: "I'd really like it if you got that college truck plugged in."

Outside, fighting stiff extension cords, ice-clogged plugs. Maybe electricity getting through, maybe not. Came inside to thaw my fingers. Stacey: "Maybe it'll work."

Sat down at computer to work on novel. Power outage.

salting a moose

It's cold here in Kotzebue. My fingers hurt and the skin is peeling; a little
frostbite. Wayne Hogue, our neighbor, is after me to write my misadven-
ture. I wrote about him last fall. The *Anchorage Daily News* editors ti-
tled my column "New white guy proves tough." He's hoping now they'll
run something along the lines of "Not-so-new white guy screws up."

Before Christmas, I got a moose, the first one in years. Bob and
Carrie had mentioned how tasty winter moose meat can be, and, jok-
ingly, I told Carrie, "Let me know if you get tired of waiting on your
husband to get one."

"I'm already tired!" she shrieked.

Bob, of course, was rethinking another subject: saline overflow,
how it froze sled dogs' feet and in high concentrations killed vegetation—in this case possibly his flower, the fringed gentian, which hadn't
returned that past summer.

Stacey decided to take the day off work to come with me to hunt for the
moose. It was mid-December, calm, and at 9:30 the ice and land lay in
morning blackness. I made coffee and checked the temperature. It was
warm enough: fifteen below zero. Nick Jans was staying at our house,
up from Juneau where he lives now, gathering signatures to get a referendum on the ballot concerning aerial wolf hunting. "Nice day," he
said. He sipped his coffee. "Wish I could *malik*."

On the drifts around the house there was fresh snow, fluffy and loose, an uncommon thing in this windstripped town. Barehanded, in light leaking from the street, I lashed a tarp and snowshoes on my freight sled. Our husky came out of his plywood box, stretched, and stood on three legs, watching wistfully and keeping a foot thawing. While the snowgo engines warmed up, I hurried inside to tell Stacey it was time to climb into the rest of our gear: parkas and fur hats, balaclava face masks and goggles, binoculars and beaver mittens.

Out beyond the edge of town we picked up the willow stakes of the Jones Trail. My headlight didn't work. In the cone of Stacey's light the snow on the sea ice glittered. Outside its cast, all the world seemed lost under darkness. Behind us dawn paled a tiny swath of sky. There were no new snowgo tracks. I gave the engine gas and raced north, gobbling up the indistinct snow. As I drove, I felt small patches of overflow sag under my track, under the snow, but we sped on without seeing sign of water.

Before the far shore we steered west and followed the coast to Uhls' spruce tree and there climbed up on the tundra. The sky had lightened. The land stretched away, rising rolling tundra dotted with clumps of brush. Through my binoculars distant willow thickets looked like patches of cropped hair. I saw no black knobs of moose, nor the wandering trail of one.

Thirty miles out, on a ridgetop, we stopped and killed the engines. The day was silent. Around us sparkled a million moth wings of frost. Far off a red yolk sun lay on the horizon of sea ice. As my binoculars went opaque, the lenses fogging from the warmth of my eyeballs, I spotted moose tracks, down in a deep creek valley. Half a mile away the black outline of two moose lay near a bank of willows.

The snow glowed in shades of pink. I forgot about big night coming and asked Stacey if she minded snowshoeing. I preferred to hunt on foot. We have a freezer in the house we rent; if we didn't get meat, oh well, there would be another day.

Snowshoeing proved to be hard work. The snow was bottomless in the creek. All did not go perfectly with the hunt, or the hunter. Another hour and more passed before the moose was down—at the bottom of a steep bluff, and in a chest-deep draw choked with willows and spruce. I was overheated from horsing my machine through thickets to get to it, getting stuck, and damp from sweat and from snow blowing up over the windshield into my face. Wisely, Stacey had waited up on the tundra.

Below the animal a creek curved, with steep cutbanks, brush, and open water. Finally I gave up on trying to break a trail in that direction. One dead moose would be going uphill through thick willows, somehow.

Up close it was the size of a Subaru, with legs. I remembered why I like caribou. And I remembered my dad rubbing his hands on the coffeepot, saying, fifteen minutes to cut up a moose. But that was back when we were out of meat. He was tough enough to run twenty miles behind his dog team, and his knife was urged on by not knowing whether moose season was open or closed.

When I cut into the skin, the moose was fat—almost like a bear— one of the fattest animals I'd seen in years. The blood was slippery from the oil. Cutting the rib joints free from the spine, my hand slipped down my knife handle, down the blade. It takes skill to cut your good hand, the one holding the knife.

Three fingers were gashed, the middle one halfway through the muscle. It wouldn't stop bleeding. Our packs on the snowgos were icy, the knotted ropes frozen. Stacey searched but couldn't find my Band-Aids. I couldn't find my electrical tape. It was getting dark, a chill falling. My thermometer read twenty below. We still hadn't even gutted the moose. Above us the bluff rose, white snow against the darkening sky, reminding us of more work waiting ahead.

Stacey cut strips out of a canvas bag, and I elevated my hand. Almost immediately the end of my finger froze. I said to hell with it, tore off the red rag. Panting and rushing, we finished the moose in twenty minutes.

My machine wouldn't start, and when it did I had to go all the way down into the creek valley to turn around. Stars had appeared overhead.

My wolf ruff was icy, my thin working gloves twisted and hard. It took three trips to haul the moose, hooves and head and everything, up onto the open tundra. Our boots felt coarse on the snow, frozen with moose blood, and nice warm blood was filling my heavy insulated glove.

The moon was up by the time we started across the tundra for home. The land glimmered, dark and silver, rolling and beautiful. I fiddled with wires under the cowling but failed to repair my headlight. We couldn't go back the way we'd come, and I navigated five miles in the moonlight before picking up our trail. As we came down from the hills, we felt the temperature dropping. My icy face mask froze my cheeks and nose, and a crosswind chilled my left side.

Finally we hit the coast, then the Jones Trail. A snowgo rocketed past, coming from town. I halted and walked back a few yards to see if Stacey was warm. She was fine but afraid of overflow. I told her we'd just passed a traveler who would have warned us if the trail was bad—but I would check. I borrowed her machine with the headlight and zipped ahead. The overflow appeared to be fine. I circled back, told her to go first, I'd follow.

She drove at a moderate speed. With no headlight, I followed close beside her, taking advantage of the light. Suddenly we were sinking. A wave went through the snow, like a baby tsunami undulating outward. It was viscous and slow, beautiful—although as we sank it was all nightmare.

I shut my engine off. Silence and night rushed in on the ice. A cold wind whispered out of the east. I stepped in. The slush and water were over my knees. "Don't panic," I told Stacey. "Don't panic." I carried a load, including my heavy camera bag, to solid ice. I waded back again for a load, and on the third trip, piggybacking her, I told her, "Something's wrong. My legs are burning."

I climbed out and ran back and forth trying to warm up. I had always believed that a good attitude was half the battle in fighting freezing. It didn't seem to be working tonight. What was wrong? Memories of Kole flashed in my head: him swimming in the ice pans to retrieve geese. I remember me diving naked under needled Breakup ice to find a friend's dropped Visegrips.

I sat on my gear bag, dug out dry spare gloves, socks, and a sweater, carried many miles since Tommy Douglas's warning. Stacey wrung out one of my boot liners. Her hands frosted instantly. We tried to dry my foot, but the water wasn't normal water. It was brine, salty, and it wouldn't come off. The wind froze my exposed skin. When I tilted my arm down, my hand started bleeding again. I started laughing. "Frig. I'm wounded *and* freezing!"

Across the ice, the line of lights reflected, as if there was more water on the trail to town. Near us in the dark a willow stabbed out of the ice, a lone trail marker. I'd planned to warm up and then to heave and inch the machines out, something I'd done many times before. But now I wasn't sure I could go back into that salt slush that felt like wading into freezing kerosene.

We tried my handheld VHF. It beeped. Cold batteries. Eventually a woman answered but couldn't make us out. I removed the batteries and warmed them under my armpit. Stacey and I hunched in the dark. "I think that was Esther Luther," Stacey said. "She's nice. What should we tell her? What should we do?"

I didn't know. I'd only carried the radio before, never called for help. When we tried it a second time, Esther pieced together syllables to understand that I wanted Jennifer Williams' boyfriend, Andrew Greene, to drive out and give us a hand; but it turned out he was at work, and then it sounded like Esther said Jennifer was coming out. "Don't let her!" I transmitted. Another radio chimed in: "Call search and rescue!"

The first voice asked for my go-ahead.

My glove was heavy. My feet freezing. I carefully placed the radio on the snow and walked directly away from it. Search and rescue was for other people, for emergencies. We could walk. But the temperature was dropping, the wind blowing a bit harder now, and we might find more "funny" water on the way. I hated to bother anyone, or to endanger them.

I sat down again and leaned on my camera bag, pulled off my cement shoepacks. Stacey lifted her parka and thawed my feet on her stomach. I glanced at the willow, our spindly companion on the moonlit ice. I could wade out, rip my seat and plastic cowling off, and make a store-bought fire. My thoughts flashed to my dad again, and I was glad he couldn't see my day of hunting. He would never dream of driving sixty miles on a snowgo to get a moose. He wouldn't go a mile. His way of hunting had mostly been to stay home; eventually all the animals came through the yard. Once, when I shot a caribou seventy yards below where Bonehead and Murphy were staked, he walked along the snowdrifts with a bucket and a knife. He was there to help but had a faint scowl on his face. "Why'd you shoot one so far from the house?" he asked.

Crossing the ice in twilight

Forty minutes later we saw the bobbing lights. Like spaceships, snow-gos roared out of the dark in snow and exhaust, noise and light, Henry Booth Jr., Steve Stein, Elvis Henry. Young guys that I'd seen around town. They brought hip boots and rope as I had requested. It took an hour to pull the machines and loaded sled out, another hour to get one of them to run. Many embarrassing minutes: stuck in the middle of what had been a fine trail; my left hand, my good hand, not much use; Stacey's scarf wrapped around my foot; my snowpants legs unzipped and flapping like ice boards.

The way those search and rescue guys worked together was impressive. After we towed the machines out of the overflow and my older snowgo wouldn't run, they pointed one of their snowgos at it, left the machine idling, and worked in the spill of the headlight. They removed the drive belt, pulled the starter hundreds of times, repeatedly dried the spark plugs. When I dismantled the fuel pump, as each tiny bolt came out, a big hand appeared out of the dark, cupped to take it. Bare hands took the diaphragm, wiped ice off the cover. No words, no whining or even a comment about twenty-below gas across their knuckles.

We left my older snowgo gray and crusted and dead on the ice beside the refreezing water. On the trail to town, running rough, a piston on my new machine blew. The price of our meat was going up.

When we got home, Stacey and I dug a hole in the snow and buried the moose to keep the meat thawed for aging. Inside, Stacey took off her heavy garments and hugged China and asked her about her day at school. It was past midnight. I called the Kotzebue emergency room. It was backed up, so I gave up on stitches for the finger that had finally stopped bleeding. Instead I headed back out on the ice with a friend to drag my dead snowgo home.

The next day we cut up the moose. The meat was fat and good. My dog, Worf, froze his pads stepping in the salt on the moose hide. Wayne came outside and helped with the work, and got some big laughs. Even Clarence Wood called on the phone to hear the story. He'd been through the ice hundreds of times and wasn't impressed. "Anyway," he said, "you learn."

Bob Uhl stopped by, for the first time ever, to assist in cutting the meat, and to hear the story. He stood in the snow, next to one of my dead snowgos, wiped his knife thoughtfully. He wasn't fazed, either. "A fat moose is so much better than a skinny one, you can afford the time to heal."

I piled fat and meat in my sled to deliver to his apartment. Inside my gloves my fingertips throbbed, itched, swelling around the nails. My middle finger was large, curved protectively, and meat showed in the cut. I handed Bob the moose nose. He politely tried to decline but then acquiesced. He grinned: "I learned through trial and error not to refuse a moose nose."

these happy spruce

In late August Raymond Hawley and I talk on the scarred and spat-upon steps of the Kivalina school. It's hard for me to believe that my dad was here, nearly fifty years ago. Still in this village are his long-ago-young friends Oran Knox and Willard Adams. Today the village of Kivalina is hunkered low, flat, wind-stripped; a waft of rancid marine mammal floats on air currents. Two Honda four-wheelers zip past, drenching us in dust. Population 375, the town is made up of HUD houses, a gymnasium, oil tanks, an airstrip, dump, and graveyard all jammed on a gravel spit only nine feet above sea level and essentially surrounded by water. It is one of the Alaska villages currently washing into a rising ocean.

Raymond is an *umialik*, a whaling captain, and he recognizes me from when I was a teenager and my family camped near his, at South Tent City, back when more than a hundred families from around the region commercial fished for salmon. Now he holds his palm up, peers at the sky. "Too hot. Not supposed to be so hot like this."

I'm in town teaching a class for Maniilaq Association, the regional Native nonprofit social services provider. I'm teaching fish canning, something that few here are interested in learning. Villagers eat plenty of fish but prefer to prepare it in traditional ways: boiled, dried, frozen raw. The school is built on beach gravel; directly behind it is the beach. Ocean stretches to the horizon in the direction of Siberia. Gravel, sand, and surf run north to Cape Thompson, where my dad lived, and south toward the Red Dog port site. Today the sea is flat, the air breathless and hot; the wire-mesh boxes of the newest multimillion-dollar erosion control project are at rest. The next storm will cause half the town to be evacuated, but we don't know that yet.

Still bright-eyed though wizened now, Raymond was a young man when the Atomic Energy Commission arrived at Ogotoruk Creek, with dozers and drills and zeal to vaporize those bird-nesting cliffs and good caribou hunting land, just for practice. He was middle-aged when Teck Cominco opened the largest lead and zinc mine in the world, across the tundra in the opposite direction. His village, more than any other village in the region—probably more than any in Alaska—has serious qualms about "progress." And it should. Recently, the AEC revealed that in 1962 they secretly buried radioactive waste at Cape Thompson. Meanwhile, the enormous tailing piles of the Red Dog strip mine leach heavy metal toxins into the Wulik River, and Cominco repeatedly violates the federal clean water and clean air acts. The Wulik empties into the sea at Kivalina; here villagers gather drinking water, hunt animals for food, and catch the Dolly Varden trout we are canning today.

"Seth," Raymond says, "this global warming, we don't know about it. There's lotta berries. *Aqpiks, paungaq.* Caribous are coming down already. Big blueberries, all over."

This still-optimistic Iñupiaq elder is not alone in questioning what the sky will bring next, or even what birds and bugs may fly in under it. All over the region people are talking of this sun-drenched summer and the crop of berries, talking of the strange occurrences of a walrus swimming upriver to Noorvik, harbor seals as far into fresh water as Onion Portage, and beluga coming at the wrong time, in midsummer, to Kotzebue Sound. Conversations are a mixture of thankfulness for these hunter-gatherer gifts and wariness of what the future will bring next.

When I'm done with my food preservation job—part-time summer employment that takes me to Kivalina and other villages—and done with salmon fishing, Stacey and China and I pack to head home up the

Blueberries on
the tundra taking
advantage of a long
and hot summer

Kobuk. Hazel Apok, my boss, says good-bye for the season and we wish each other a good fall. She's a middle-aged Iñupiaq woman, small and kind and wise to the ways of the white world and Eskimo alike. Her black hair has a little gray beginning to show around the temples, likely a result of too many hours poring over Bureau of Indian Affairs reports and Bureau of Land Management mining proposals—a rising tide of paper that she works tirelessly to decipher for Maniilaq. Originally from Kiana, Hazel speaks in a voice full of envy that I'm heading upriver. Her eyes glowing, she talks of blueberry patches she's been spending time in. She pauses, grows contemplative. "It seems like the Lord gives us all kinds of blessings right before times of hardship. That's what the elders used to say."

I walk away pondering her words. In this, the Store-Bought Age, misgiving is no new emotion for me. I recall Hannah Newlin, old and in a wheelchair, tending flowers with me at the Senior Center, telling stories of famine and influenza, of dog-team travelers finding half-starved children in igloos full of frozen dead people. And I wonder who among us remembers such hardship.

My wife and daughter and I travel by boat, and the Kobuk is dried up, as low as I've ever seen it; some of the sandbars have a green tinge: grass. Inside a slough we find abandoned beaver dams—dry on both sides—the grass high and healthy in the trench of the former waterway. Possibly drainage ceased here because of the permafrost melting, we don't know. Near a pond I poke my head through the willows. Where geese usually land the mud is now overgrown. Equisetums have gone crazy, deep and thick and neon-green as fishing lures—something out of *Jurassic Park.*

On the river in front of our house, Stacey and China help push our wooden boat over shallows to get ashore, and we carry loads up the hill. It is evening, still pleasant and warm, sixty degrees along the bank. There has been no frost yet, nothing close. We used to expect a frost in mid or late August; early September often brought the first snow, the tundra brilliant white under laden clouds. Now berries hang on bushes where I didn't know bushes grew, even under my dad's log cache. I eat a few hundred, glancing out over the tundra for caribou. The berries are delicious, but something about the tundra doesn't look right.

There has always been low brush behind our sod igloo, but this summer's crop has been the steroid kind, disconcerting. Caribou could come through those dwarf birch, willows, and alders, sure, but I'm not going to spot them instantly the way I used to. I mutter to Stacey, "Maybe I better order high-heels."

The fireweed and stinkweed, poplar and highbush cranberries all smell of fall, a good smell and full of memories, and we head up the trail to open the house. The trail in front of the igloo has sunk two feet vertically. The entire front of the hill has simply dropped—permafrost melting underground. Inside, winged ants have been eating the spruce ridgepoles. Their sawdust and bug carcasses lie in heaps on the floor. We sweep them up and build a fire to warm the chilly subterranean room. If I'd never seen a television, never heard of global warming or the bird flu or the honey bee crisis, I'd still be superstitious with these strange changes—now I'm troubled about the bugs eating the house and the hill sinking, and that vision of the tundra making me wonder how I'll spot meat, which we need. I try to recall how this hill and land looked in the past. I dig in a drawer, searching through my parents' abandoned photos. The scent of mold rises. I brush aside mouse droppings, pry apart curled prints: a photo of Kole and me barefoot and smiling over bowls of bear fat, another of Alvin with us skinning beavers. I hold slides up to light leaking in between leaves on the trees outside the windows. Finally, I find the one I'm looking for. In pencil on the cardboard frame is my mom's neat handwriting: *Sept. 1965. Anore, Don, and Howie in front of the cache.*

They stand below Howie's new log cache. Such young and handsome pioneers! They appear to be headed somewhere—to gather firewood, or bring home meat. Behind them tundra stretches to the north. Open tundra. Tundra that nowadays is head-high brush and green

Anore, Don, and Howard, 1965 (Photo by Erna Kantner)

China playing below the old cache; the tundra to the north growing in with trees, 2007

spruce. And even I, a believer, catch my breath: this climate change is as old as I am. Probably older.

On the stove a kettle begins to sing. Memories of Ole Wik rise in my head—him standing in front of their igloo on a snowdrift, tall and thin, one leg shorter than the other, straight blond hair. He taught Kole and me card games and mind puzzles. Way back when we were kids playing tag with slingshots loaded with rabbit turds and experimenting with saltpeter and non-dairy creamer, Ole had handy his serious adult talk too—warnings of a future of overpopulation and the greenhouse effect. Later, in high school and at college there were questions on exams about CO_2 in the atmosphere. But America, I found out, wasn't Ole and Sasha's igloo. The greenhouse effect was whiny, wimpy environmentalist talk, not cool to my college acquaintances, Ohio relatives, and Eskimo hunting companions alike.

Forty years, twenty, ten—somewhere along these decades there has been a turning, an infiltration so gradual and huge that it has leapfrogged awareness and arrived at acceptance. We have no glamorous glaciers here calving into the sea cataloging climate change like the ones we see in the documentaries. Polar bears and their problems— until recently—have been hundreds of miles north, invisible to us who are busy roaming our own familiar trails. It's the small things that we notice; with our eyes and fingers touching food from the land we come back with questions: Why is the tundra so blue with berries, and will we pay for those sweets with no caribou this year, or a village washed away? Or worse, companions drowned?

Looking back, now I can see one of the tremors on the fault line of climate change, a bright night in May 1999, the night Doug Sheldon and Raymond Brown disappeared.

Doug, sixty-nine or seventy, seasoned and tough and a lifelong reindeer herder, was out hunting on the sea ice, an environment where he was experienced and a renowned marksman. His companion, Raymond, was six or eight years younger, a dog musher, hunter, and father of six kids. He too had vast experience on the sea ice and like

Doug was connected to the region by a trellis of relatives and ancestors.

It was a spring evening of the kind we love and pay dearly for in Darkness, winter, and storm. Folks were out hooking sheefish, traveling between villages, hunting caribou; night and snow both were almost gone for another season, the sun at midnight barely setting behind the mountains.

I was out that night with a shotgun, hoping to spot an early goose. Crossing a pond, my snowgo sank in a moat forming along the edge of the ice. Stuck, chilled, wet to the thighs, I spent hours heaving my machine up to a hump of frozen ground—nothing out of the ordinary for any tested spring traveler. I drained my boots and carburetors, changed to a dry drive belt, and inched home across ice grayed in fog. Thawing out beside the stove, listening to Johnson Greene on KOTZ radio, I heard that a search was on. Not another search for partying delinquents lost on the trail or goose hunters out of gas, but this time for two elders traveling together out on the wide open sea ice. Somewhere out on Kotzebue Sound were Raymond Brown and Doug Sheldon.

Raymond had been the Friends Church pastor in Ambler when Alvin and I hunted geese on the Breakup ice. On snowgo and by boat, he stopped at our place along the river to visit. He, like my parents, brought his family to the coast to commercial fish every summer. He couldn't hear well and had an easy smile, which he used when he missed a piece of the conversation. His son, Jimmy, had been one of Alvin's best friends; I'd been jealous when the family took Alvin with them to the coast to hunt seals. Doug's wife, Tessie, worked at Maniilaq, and I saw her every time I walked into the building; Doug had gotten turnip seeds from me at my food preservation job and in the conversation convinced me to buy a .25-06, the caliber of rifle I now use. I realized that I—second-generation white kid or not—was part of the fabric of this region that these men were so much a part of.

They had left Cape Krusenstern on snowgos, dragging hardwood basket sleds loaded with camping gear and tools for hunting seals, prized for oil and meat even in this age of box pizzas and beefsteaks at

Following pages:
The reflection of
open ocean on
winter sky

Alaska Commercial, prized especially by the old people, tied to the past by food from the land. They carried warm clothing, VHF radios, spare gas; Doug had a kayak lashed on top of his load. They intended to find the edge of the fast ice, roughly thirty miles out from town, somewhere in a line between Sealing Point and Cape Espenberg. For centuries their ancestors hunted this same familiar icescape.

Days passed. The men didn't appear out of the fog as everyone expected, nor were they spotted stranded on ice floes. No call came on the VHF. The warming spring days were met by west wind off the sea; fog rolled in and out of Kotzebue Sound. Soon the search became all-out, in the badlands of shifting spring ice, slush, and open leads. Searchers on snowgos roamed the ice as far as they dared. Local pilots in small planes flew assigned sectors over the ocean. The Coast Guard was called in, and day after day their C-130 droned over the sound, flying crisscross patterns along the coast and far out to sea. No trace was ever found. These elders, with their combined decades of hunter-gatherer knowledge, their intermingling in the lives of nearly everyone in the region, were gone.

Death is an accepted part of life in Iñupiaq culture. Between suicides, old age, and accidents out on the land, death is all too common. In the shock and loss we didn't recognize that it might not have been Doug and Raymond's expertise and vast experience that had failed them.

The intervening years have cast the incident in a different light. Now the names are piling up—Dan Snyder Sr., Diane Nelson, David Keith, Boris McLuke, Stanley Custer Jr., and more—these days all of us have relatives or friends drowned through weak ice, thin ice, refrozen ice. Word has trickled down from Barrow that their midwinter sea ice has lost predictability and is hardly related to the terrain of generations past. Kivalina and Shishmaref are washing out to sea, beach erosion caused by longer ice-free seasons. The trail crossing between Kotzebue and Deering has been all but abandoned because of open leads and uncertain ice, and hunters and travelers have grown accustomed to extended Freezeups, complicated by thaws and by rain in late October and November. And we have become familiar with that ominous black cloud on the horizon—the reflection of open ocean on winter sky.

Now, I rise and put away memories—of futile days on frighteningly unsafe ice, searching for a friend, David Keith, lost crossing from the mouth of the Noatak. I put away my parents' pictures and step outside into evening. I haul an armload of firewood for night. The sun has set behind those mountains in the west toward Kiana. The air is still warm. Strangely, no gnats or no-see-ums swarm out of the weeds to bite my wrists and temples. Across the tundra, the fall colors glow in yellows and burgundy. Even the north wind is not blowing, here where it so seldom ceased in my younger life. Ironically, warmth, on the surface at least, is not hard to accept. Especially in the Arctic. With it, I'm afraid, we may have to accept many other things: funerals not just for people but also for whole species and foods and familiar ways we love—such as traveling on ice. Yet a hungry land forces acceptance of what the land serves up. From my dad's stories of Mabel and Austin up at Cape Thompson, I know that he admired the old Eskimos' optimism in facing an uncertain tomorrow, and before dusk I walk back down the trail to his log cache, to eat a few more sweet irresistible berries before they freeze, and to look again at those happy trees spreading across the tundra to the north.

silver strangers

On our counter a pearl-blue ten-pound trout is thawing. Outside, it is the ocean that should be frozen, but slush rains out of the sky. The far shore of the lagoon slowly goes white as I roll up Helly Hansen rain gear and stash orange wristlets behind my Ice King shoepacks. Hip boots can't be stored outside either; they'll freeze and crack, and when water reappears after winter they'll be as useful as those flat salmon carcasses along the sandbars.

I shelve net nettles and hanging twine, too. Salmon season seems a dream now, with big Arctic darkness coming our way. Even spring this past year was white and cold, much of May below freezing, and snowstorms in June. Geese and ducks and songbirds arrived; they huddled, chilled and waiting for enough warmth to make families. It all added up to mistrust in the sky, a reality now in climate-changing northwest Alaska, and left locals wondering when and if salmon would come home.

Fishing gets in your blood, though, and in July I biked down to South Tent City, a mile down the shore from the house we rent in Kotzebue, to get my nets prepared. Stacey and China came along, as did Worf, the thirdhand dog, working his way around a dredge and dozers, the Kikiktagruk Native corporation digging up gravel.

Above the pebbles, beach grass swayed in the breeze. Stacey and I opened our wall tent, where I've lived more of my summers than anywhere else. It smelled like mildew and nets, dried seaweed and ground squirrel possessions. We stacked out three shackles of gear, taking time to mend winter mouse chews and last season's seal tears in the web. Overhead, seagulls slipped downwind, eyeing our activity and crying approval of anything related to fish. Mosquitoes swarmed, thirsty and undeterred by snowdrifts lining the shore. China, nine years old now, lit a smudge fire to keep them away.

She's little and lithe, and the age I was when I started commercial fishing. Back then my family fished before and after the commercial season, of course, to feed us and our dog team for the winter. We used gill nets and seines, and had little cash, time, or feeling for fiddling with a pole and single monofilament line, casting three-dollar lures into current. The closest we came to that was a section of willow and twine—jigging grayling and mudshark through the ice at night in November.

At South Tent City, Stacey and China and I finished preparing the nets and stood for a while on the snowdrifts and stared out over the water. Offshore white dots—icebergs—glinted on the horizon, keeping question in the air. Word was, Iñupiaq whalers up the coast at Point Hope were still shorebound, after months of waiting for open leads.

A few days later, boating home from searching the melting cliffs for Pleistocene ivory, we motored up in front of my tent. We decided to set a net. The girls held the buoy line snubbed off in the bow while I towed fifteen floats worth of web into the water. Nothing hit, no splashes, no tails, no bobbing corks. The outgoing current was strong.

In the morning a couple of friends came with us to check the net. There was a simple excitement in the air, at the possibility of first salmon. Trying to get the maximum entertainment—and burn the least gas—we didn't drive my fishing boat all the way around out of the lagoon, but took four-wheelers and carried an air mattress. I paddled out on my chest and released the outer anchor. Stacey and China and our friends pulled the lead line and cork line, stacking the net onshore.

Fish flopped out of the water, and shouting started, whoops and whistles. I flailed back to the beach and climbed out in time to assist. From in front of the next tent down, a girl swam our way; her grandma

Seth picking salmon
out of the net at the
Noatak bar

followed, hurrying down the beach; she asked about fresh salmon heads—a favorite of Iñupiat and my parents alike. July 6, and I was handing out beautiful chum salmon, high in oil content, excellent eating, seemingly a different creature from the poor-quality chums in the lower part of the state where waters are warmer.

We have long winters, plenty of time to get tired of each other and each other's conversations, and of caribou, and cold, and then there arrives these silver strangers we remember fondly. Fourth of July and salmon traditionally come the same week in Kotzebue Sound, and inside of me is an emotion—something between awe, love, and disbelief—for this combination of nature's predictability and generosity.

The commercial season opened the second week of July. My dad and I set out a few days later. So near the beginning of the run, we only hoped to pay for gas. But we both like to be out on the water, fishing, and we are more relaxed working than relaxing. He's seventy-two and still climbing trees and mountains, leaping in and out of the boat, pulling 900 feet of gear without resting. For that third, six-hour opener of the season I expected fifty fish at best. But salmon started hitting while we were still setting net over the stern—a good sign. Howie loves to watch the net. Especially when it's splashing.

We caught 375, and the following week, still early in the season, 2,000 more, directly in front of my tent, a mile from town, in five feet of water.

Our fishery has been in doubt, tenuous, and in decline for twenty years. Prices have been fifteen to twenty cents a pound, one-third what they were three decades ago. In those intervening years costs for gas and everything else has climbed fivefold and tenfold. In 2001 Tom Monson, our local buyer, couldn't make the numbers work and announced that he wouldn't be buying.

As always, I wanted to fish. I wasn't frantic, just relentless. I leased Tom's loader, found a Seattle buyer, and became their agent. In my boat

I wore a noose I never thought I'd wear, a cell phone tied around my neck with net-hanging twine. During the season I slept four-hour nights, fished as always but now also dealt with freight schedules and canceled flights, broken ice machines, leaky totes, and upset fisherman whom I couldn't buy from because my operation was too small to handle more than my catch and my partner's. For two seasons my net was cut by more props than in the previous thirty years. My partner and I were the only ones in the water, and I too would have been jealous.

Then along came a federal grant, to establish a buyer; the money was to encourage small business. Typical of government, the first casualty was my small business; the second, mismanagement of the funds, until they were gone. During that time I began selling a portion of my catch here locally, three salmon here, six there. It hasn't been a gold mine, except in satisfaction. It makes me happy to catch a beautiful salmon a mile or two from town, bleed it, ice it, and give some grandma, doctor, or pilot the best fish possible. It's a short season, good feelings, and then I'm on to other things, all of course designed around the goal of avoiding a steady job that might interfere with next season's fishing.

All in all this season was good; I missed a bunch of the best of it due to other commitments, but that was okay too. My parents left at the end of July, to go visit Kole and his wife and kids in Seattle, and then head on home to their little coffee farm on the Big Island of Hawaii. I fished on without a partner. I've done it before, and even once hauled in 1,200 fish in seven hours, but it is tough in the wind and waves, and not without danger; no one is going to steer around and rescue you if you end up over the side tangled in your gear. This year, though, I've mellowed (or gotten wiser?) with age and I cut back to one shackle, 300 feet of net.

Summer was gray. Many of the openers were 5:00 to 11:00 a.m. Mornings, I crept out of the lagoon at 4:00 a.m. in darkness and drizzle. I went east, shhh. . . ! to my secret spot; along the bar. Actually, half of the twenty or thirty boats left in the fishery head toward the mouth of the river in August.

Across from the tundra bluffs, I idled in shallows and dark, my motor inhaling silt while I tried to fathom which way was water, which way more mud. I dropped anchor and set as grayness lifted. Canada geese were honking above the fog, and the gleeful cries of gulls and swans drifted out of the dawn and shallows north of my buoy. Half a mile down-channel Gus Nelson's net came alive, hammering salmon, making me feel crippled with such a short net. Regardless, it was great to meet the morning on the water.

Salmon tangled in the webbing

Just when the August weather is growing rough, the midnight sun has gone, and the salmon are declining, along swims something even more dazzling and tasty: the Dolly Varden trout run.

This August, before putting the nets away and heading up the Kobuk to my old home, I still had orders in town for a few salmon and for all the trout I could catch. It's not easy to catch trout without catching five or ten times as many salmon. As it happened, a group of writers and photographers flew in and wanted a boat ride across to Sisualik. The group included Nick, so I agreed to take them. Of course I took a section of net, too.

While they visited and interviewed the Uhls, I ran my web out from shore. Fish hit immediately, slow but steady. I worked back and forth, picking fish and putting them in what ice I had. That thirdhand dog of mine was along, hanging his lips over the bow. He loves fish. Nick, too, smelled the action, grabbed his waders, and waved me ashore. We pulled in eighteen salmon—a couple reds and silvers—and fifteen or so trout. The trout were that pearl blue, lit up like sky, smooth and fat and perfect. Thankfully, there weren't any twenty-plus-pounders that are too big to grab around the tail and too miraculous for me not to try to release them. They do give me a chuckle though, wondering how many times I and others might have baked the state record.

When the writers climbed in for the ride home they lamented leaving their fly rods in town. I didn't know what to tell them about whether these trout would bite now, here in the ocean. I hardly know a fishing rod from a tent pole. I did mention how good they tasted.

Tonight, one of those fish is coming out of the oven. And come summer, I'll be back on the coast, stacking net, getting prepared to be gilled again in this fishery, more addiction than career.

the whiteboy award

Kobuk Lake was west wind this fall, rough crossing. I came down from
Kapikaġvik on September 24. It was cold and clear; spray froze when it
hit the deck. I should have tied my load better before leaving the mouth
of Melvin Channel. It would have been good to have a companion,
someone to bail the boat and shift the weight a little toward the stern.
Worf was with me; poor guy, fur soaked even under the collar, and trying to brace for each plunge. He got sick, vomited on the floorboards. I
couldn't stop—I had to keep my eyes on the bow going down and those
curling waves coming up.

The left side of the boat was iced when we got into the lagoon in
Kotzebue. The first boat that passed, the driver stared. Wind gusted
dark cat paws on the water. I was glad it wasn't freezing over. My face
was stiff, legs and shoulders, too. Worf inched along the deck and
leaped ashore; he was happy to get out and sniff around and piss. Me,
I had to unload. I threw the bow and stern anchors, snubbed them off,
and started tossing empty gas jugs ashore.

Stacey and China ran out in boots and jackets, wind messing up
their hair. I pried off my raincoat before hugging them. Chilled, and
standing there in leaky hip boots, I could hear waves grinding the chine
of my wooden boat into the gravel. "Let's unload," I said.

China grabbed gas jugs and carried them between the houses.
"Seth, stop a second," Stacey said. "I've got some big news."

China Kantner
and Gabbi Gregg
picking berries

I turned away, jumped in over the gunnel, handed out white plastic buckets of cranberries. "Here. Boat's grinding. Let's unload."

"Some guy called, with this distinguished accent. They want to give you an award. The Whiting Award."

"Good. Balance this caribou a minute."

Stacey's face lit up. "You got caribou! Fat meat? Did you get it on the way downriver, or at home?"

It wasn't easy to talk after being alone for days and then traveling all day on the water. And I needed time and privacy—a corner of a cabin with family all outside—to unwrap the news of this mysterious gift. "Who's this wants to give me a whiteboy award?"

"It's the Whiting Writers' Award. It comes with a huge prize. They want to fly you to New York City to receive it."

I lifted a caribou butt to shore, fat and clean and still in the skin to protect the meat. I set it on a clean canvas tarp, straightened my back. "I don't want to go to New York."

I climbed back in the boat. Grabbed my camera bag and .25-06 and handed them out. "I already went to New York City. Twice." I paused, turned, pointing above the horizon. "They don't have their whole sky, just little strips. I have to go to Minneapolis in a couple days. And the paperback tour is next month, to how many frigging cities. Here's my rifle—careful, I'm trying to keep the salt spray off of it."

On the jet, it was that trapped-in-a-tube type of travel. Strapped in seats, blind view ahead, someone else driving. No spare caribou hindquarter allowed, no rifle, no knife or even matches—a naked way to cross America. My leg hurt, the one that got run over by Howie and Keith's Yukon sled when I was four. My stomach hurt from a year of too many book readings, the courage to speak in front of strangers sponsored by too much coffee and alcohol. In the seats beside me China and Stacey sat, coloring and doing a crossword puzzle, happy to be going on a trip.

The Newark, New Jersey, airport was busy; cars and buses sped away and always there were more pouring up to the curb. We stood in a quick-moving line and bought taxi tickets to Manhattan. Out on the roads, the driver found the route—amazing to me, but if he came up north on the tundra in winter probably he'd say the same. He steered around long trucks the way Alvin and I would boat around ice pans coming downriver. Except this metal river moved ten or fifteen times the speed of the Kobuk and squirted down concrete channels—nowhere to climb ashore and pick wild onions or glass for bears.

In the back seat, I pinched China's smooth little neck. I squeezed my fingers between my pocket and the seat cushion, to make sure I hadn't lost my only tool to shelter her and find food—my Visa card. I hoped it continued to have its magic for another few days.

The cab driver stopped at a red light. He leaned back. "Alaska, huh. How cold is it up there?"

"The ocean is freezing over," I said.

He peered out his window at the side mirror. "I couldn't live like that."

"People get used to different things," I said.

The driver gunned forward, swerved in behind a cement truck. He was all done with Alaska questions and now back to his world: the buses and bicycles, horns and lights and crowds of New York City.

We stayed at the Library Hotel. Books were on shelves in the lobby. China and Stacey enjoyed reading titles on the elevator and along the hallways. Stacey is a librarian; she'd heard of the place, and staying there was an honor. Libraries give me headaches. I tried to go outside but the door I opened dropped seven stories down steep metal mesh stairs, a near vertical fire escape. Down below, the street was moving and loud.

We walked to a restaurant, an expensive one. Inside, it was hard to hear. It had been a long two days flying here. At the table China cried briefly and then wiped her tears. "It's too loud, Dad. Everything here's too loud." The food was good although my steak was a little bit rotten. I told the waiter, "No offense, I just know rotten meat. I've seen a lot of it." The waiter had seen a lot of New York City, a human metropolis like no other. He probably thought I should be getting a national award not for writers but for nuts.

The next day we had fun roaming the subways and streets, Central Park, Chinatown. In the evening a car came for us. A lady on the phone referred to it as a limo, which was glamorous until it turned out to be a van, not a long sleek black car like Elvis or my alleged distant cousin Paul Kantner the rock-star rode in. The driver took us down tall-sided streets that were starting to look familiar. Stacey and China were dressed up and looked beautiful. I pulled at my jeans, flicked some lint on the floor, and stared out the window, wondering what the caribou were doing, right then, up north.

We were ushered into a building, down a hall, to a room with chairs and people. I recognized some of them. Chip Blake, a former editor of mine, had driven hours down the city-choked coast to be there. Hilary Reeves and Emily Cook from my publisher had flown in from Minnesota. Everyone was fancy. Uncomfortable, I glanced down at my shoes, noticed a caribou-blood stain on my cuff. Hilary bent close and manufactured some fiction: "Kantner, you look great." I glanced at a door, wistfully.

Robert L. Belknap, a tall, elderly man, spoke. He was humorous and debonair, like an East Coast father in a movie, not like any fathers in my life. He made us all laugh, and his accent was pleasant to listen to even when I wasn't paying attention to his words. He explained how Whiting Award recipients were chosen based on their writing and on the committee's belief in that writer's future work, not on skin color or who your friends or parents were. I liked that; I wasn't used to that. Stacey nudged me. "That's him! That's the accent from the phone call."

When Belknap got to me on the list, my education sounded feeble compared to the others'. He might as well have stuck with "Seth Kantner is good at skinning wolverine feet." When our group photo was taken there were nine women and men dressed in suit jackets and pretty clothes. Standing slightly apart from the group was me in jeans and my best brown Banana Republic T-shirt.

All of us received envelopes and a thick black book—literature—published by the Library of America. Mine was Melville, three novels bound together, including *Moby-Dick*, a story I'd never been able to get through. I held onto it nervously; I'd just won a huge literary award and I believed it necessary to get out of the building before anyone asked my opinion of Melville, or any other literary figure. *How do you like Dostoyevsky? Uh, is that vodka, or a salad dressing?* The fact that the Whiting people had liked my writing enough to single me out—all the way from this building, among these thousands of buildings, thousands of miles away from my life at the other end of America—seemed like a mistake. *Come on, Stacey; get your jacket, China—we have to get out of here before someone realizes I'm more about campfires and caribou soup.*

On the street that night we were happy and starting to enjoy the bizarre New York City feel. Stacey and China and I walked the few blocks to Times Square. The crowds were not threatening now, and we were getting slightly accustomed to the noise. There was so much light under the night sky it was like a bubble of day. People filled the sidewalks. Horses clomped past, pulling carriages; yellow taxis passed. I angled between people on and off the curb. Suddenly Stacey shouted. I turned. I stood practically on the toes of my old boss, Chester Ballot, a tall, slim Eskimo man from Kotzebue. A few yards away, on the other side of a stream of strangers, Bish Gallahorn, also from Kotzebue, leaned against the stone wall of a skyscraper, talking into a cell phone. We laughed and stared around at the herds of people from around the planet. How did we from the same small dot in the Arctic bump into each other here in this city? Chester worked in Kotzebue in tribal services, for Maniilaq, a nonprofit Native corporation; Bish was president of the Kikiktaugruk Native corporation.

"Chester? What are you doing here?"

He smiled big. "What are *you* doing here?"

We shook hands. They had been at a conference in Connecticut and had taken the train down, to see Times Square. Crowds flowed past, disinterested. I felt like some kind of minnow that had been moved to Mars—yet somehow recognized another fish. It was good to see those guys. We said a few more words. Moments later they disappeared, into that other America.

One more long cab ride and we arrived back at the Newark Airport: 6:45 a.m. The sun was coming up, sickly through smoke-gray horizons, red and far across miles and miles of smokestacks and buildings. It was an unforgettable vision—a warning of what human endeavor can do to the land. We were hungry, and waited in line at an airport restaurant. The scrambled eggs, hash browns, and toast didn't have the right amount of flavor; the orange juice tasted like it had been stored in stovepipe. Eighteen dollars, and we left most of the food. I was thankful to hurry aboard the plane and squeeze into the blind row of seats pointed northwest.

Back on the ground in Kotzebue the gravel was hard, frozen. Wisps of snow blew down the shore ice. A freezing rain had recoated my boat in ice. The tarps had blown off my dad's old basket sled and I could see where stanchions needed replacing and the whole sled needed a coat of pine tar and turpentine.

Our caribou meat was crusted in ice, partially frozen, but aged nicely and ready to cut. China went to school, Stacey bundled up in warm clothes and walked to work. I spread cardboard and sharpened knives. I carried in the first hindquarter, and flipped on KOTZ radio for company. Roasts and soupbones were heaped here and there when Alaska Public Radio Network came on. *Alaskan author Seth Kantner was recently named one of the nation's top ten emerging writers by the Whiting Foundation. Kantner received a forty thousand dollar prize in New York City. . . .*

Oh, shit.

I'd never been interested in being rich; but worse was to *not* be rich and thought of as such. My book had taken twelve years to write and had earned me as much as a truck driver made at Red Dog in a summer.

In my head I heard Nelson Greist, talking after Keith and Anore moved to California to work as caretakers on a ranch. Years before that Anore had researched and written a book on edible plants; she'd spent years and Maniilaq had paid her a flat three thousand dollars. "She get how much million for tat pook. They gonna California."

In the morning, at the post office strangers and friends alike were talking about the prize. Greg Garrett stood in his big shoepacks at the front of the line, picking up a package. He swiveled slowly and smiled in his beard. "Writerboy!" People laughed and congratulated me. "Hey, I sure need new snowgo," a man joked. Or maybe he wasn't joking.

"My Honda's running funny," a woman said. Someone asked for four thousand, for a boob job. I slunk back to the house, finished cutting the meat, packed my camping gear and cameras and headed home, out of town.

Seth making coffee while waiting on caribou (Photo by Nick Jans)

watching for mammoth

A couple of miles upriver from home I swing our old plywood boat in toward shore. What's been on my mind today is a hike, and picking cranberries before too many leaves cover them, and maybe getting a goose before the flocks go south. But now suddenly I'm wishing to see Silver Dollar Lake and remembering a story Kole told about mammoth bones back there.

It's a steady rain day on the Kobuk, the water high and muddy with sticks coming down the current black as swimming beavers. This rainy fall has embedded its gray melancholy in my head; the steady drip off lacy birch branches and down the sod walls of my house has matched the drip of light leaving the Arctic, again. After so many seasons what I feel toward the coming Darkness is hard to name; some emotional relative to resentment, maybe a sign of age approaching, maybe too much frostbite passed. Today is a day before snow, a day for a hike to a favorite spot, maybe to touch the bones of the ancients.

Stacey gets out when I nudge the bow into shore at the upper end of Paungaqtaugruk bluff. She anchors the boat. Jim Dau, our visiting friend, wades into the willows. He wears Alaskan dress shoes: Xtra-tuff rubber boots. The leaves are yellow and scarred brown and wet, the grass too, but if it were dry as July he'd still be wearing those Xtra-tuffs. And me, I am worse, a hip boot hiking fool.

We scrabble up the sheer stony face of Paungaqtaugruk and stop to huff at the top. Spruce cover the ridge and draws like a black wolf ruff. We stand breathing in the awe of the big river down below and the history of that river carved and abandoned, carved and abandoned in loops of lake and timber, willows and swamp all layered away south toward the Waring Mountains. A bull moose stands far out on a fling of tawny grass. His burnished antlers glint across the distance. In willows near the bull a cow feeds. I glass for geese. It is almost noon and there are none. The flocks will be out in the blueberries, or maybe gone south. I guess that the luck-a-lucks have passed, the Canadas still around. All this loud rain, I haven't been able to listen to the land.

In the trees a faint bear and human trail meanders along the precipice then angles north. The air dims and smells of slimy leaves, spruce branches, and squirrels' cone-chip piles. After the climb up the bluff the dank forest gets us peering about, exhilarated, alive, listening and breathing like animals eligible to be eaten. I tug at my homemade glove holster under my arm. It is not a quick apparatus, more the handiwork of a bush utilitarian who has no desire to pay for a store-bought holster. One with superstitious belief that the bear should have at least a share of the odds.

The spruce shrink. The alders grow thick and tall. The air is hushed; finally all dripping has ceased. We come to a sapling worn smooth and brown with missing bark, knobby with the pitch scabs of a wounded spruce. As far back as I can recollect, this particular tree has suffered the abuse of bears. I glance at the path ahead and then bend close to check the news. Dark brown hairs are here, and fresh white claw punctures, seven or eight feet off the ground. Possibly a good-sized male brown bear passed within the last day or two. Possibly I think I'm smart and only a teenage bear stood on tiptoes, way back at the beginning of the rains. I should ask Stacey's opinion; she has a keener eye for details. But this close to open tundra I cringe at talk contaminating our approach to animals.

We walk on. The alders part. Suddenly tundra is under our feet, a vast and stunning sweep of crimson, huge enough to halt breath. Just as quickly, the trail has vanished. Stacey and Jim and I stand silent among tall tussocks, glancing back to mark the path already invisible in the line where miles of grassy heads meld with miles of brush. The sky is lifting. The Jade Mountains tower in front, bold blue pyramids reaching into cloud.

A black mound a hundred yards out catches our eyes. I hunch instinctively, raise my binoculars. Jim is doing the same. But this is no bear; it is something human-made. We walk out to a pile of sod squares that appear to have been stacked by summer Bureau of Land Management workers, marking the survey corner of a Native allotment. After a lifetime growing up on this wind-bitten bluff, the fear that survey tape shivers through me is stronger than any ninety-below storm. I have flown over the States all parceled and owned in squares. I have traveled the confines of those straight, straight roads. Quickly, I lead the others northeast, away into the endless offering of tundra. Stacey is originally from Boston, Jim from Michigan. She is my wife, he a close friend, yet how their eyes see this wild land I am never exactly sure. I'm from here, Paungaqtaugruk, nowhere else, and in one way I'm like the animals: people will always frighten me most.

The sun pokes through pimples in the gray and lights the land. The tundra gradually rises as we walk. For a mile and more this rise goes on, tempting us with a view as tundra ridges often do, only to crown to another flat horizon, seducing our feet to another thousand steps over the tussocks, boots slipping off grass heads, bending blueberry bushes, tripping in the boggy hollows in between. I work my way through a scattering of brush and peer down at a pile of bear scat, damp and purple and speckled with leaves. The surface is not rain-pocked. My skin wakes muscles I've forgotten. It is precious to be alive.

I look back to see the others, twenty and thirty yards back, bent and eating berries. Blueberries snag my attention. I move on. Still the ridge will not crown. The clouds have stretched and broken into furrows. Sunlight beams down. Under my feet, bearberry leaves glow bright as blood from a dying caribou's lungs. Dwarf birch leaves shine tiny orange lights, and blueberry leaves beneath them fall red and pink and brown on the carpet of Labrador tea and pale yellow and green lichens. Near a bleached caribou antler, gnawed by wolverines and porcupines, I pause to eat *pauṅġaqs*, blueberries, cranberries, and to inhale the aromatic buffet of tundra in fall glory.

Another thousand steps and the land drops away. On the enormous plain there is no mistaking the bear. The brown bear is almost black. He grazes on berries, maybe a mile away. Distances here lose definition; a potentially dangerous animal feels close, and that matters more than a number. In the great bowl below, Silver Dollar sprawls like a mile-wide mirror dropped from the pocket of a passing giant. I glance at the ridgetop for other bears and then glass the lake for geese. They are out there, a large flock swimming for the safety of the middle. In the binoculars the brown bear's head is massive, his body rounded yet long—no three-year-old "teenage" bear, but an elder. I scrutinize him, then my gaze swings away as I scan for other creatures. I feel dislodged from modern times, looking down at a prehistoric landscape, my eyes straining to spot a herd of mammoth that must be out there on the grassy plain.

Beyond the lake, the expanse stretches north to the Jades, west over a rise and down into the timbered Hunt River valley, and on. To the east the land rolls and folds and eventually rises to the high tundra ridge that runs to Onion Portage; this ridge is the land's gentle rudder, every fall steering a cascade of caribou south to plunge into the water at the same crossing hunted by Eskimos nine thousand years ago.

Birch and aspen dot the miles, their trunks chalky white and leaves splashes of yellow. Behind us to the south the Waring Mountains march east toward the hazy blue Rabbit Mountains and those in turn taper to Old Man Mountain, hunched and guarding the edge of the earth.

Small groups of caribou graze beside us, and behind now, too. A line of a hundred or more bulls moves across the flats, angling around the far shore of the lake. Other herds dot the landscape, the white of their manes catching light like distant quartz outcroppings flung across the ocean of tundra.

I kneel and sit on a grassy tussock, wait for the others, and remember what life lets me often forget, that this is one of my favorite places.

Caribou coming out
of the mountains,
working their way
toward Onion
Portage

When they arrive, day packs pat the ground softly. We speak in murmurs, of antiquity, mammoths, and the time of cave bears. We sit for long minutes gazing, gazing back five, ten, a hundred thousand years. The feeling swallows chatter. The ancients left something here. The silence suggests that soon they may return. Camels and bison, dwarf horses and sloths, saber-toothed tigers, mastodons and men. What lives walked this valley? Who hunted whom? What thousand passions played and faded here?

The bear stands, a hulking nine-foot wall of hairy hunter. He whiffs the passing caribou. He drops on all fours facing a tangent that will miss us to the right. The herd bunches and stops. The bear charges. Bull caribou rear up and spill away, signaling alarm. The animals skim across the tussocks. The bear follows, his fat body sloshing. I think about how good his meat would taste. Finally he stops and watches the caribou flee as if they all have played this teasing game before. The bear eats more berries, occasionally charging another small herd. The distance between us has halved, but he's moving east too, no longer between us and the lake. Still, at charging speed he could be pulling off my hip boots in ninety seconds or so. We wait.

After a while we start the last mile down to the lake. We squelch through swampy draws. I carry Stacey across a rivulet. Finally we reach the good-walking lichen ridges on the east side of Silver Dollar. The geese are suspicious and paddle far across the water, near the northwest shore now. The bear leans back to the berries, a distant dot roving east. I stare out at the untouchable geese and appreciate his wistful hunger. We open our packs and spread out cheese, pilot crackers, *paniqtuq*, and chocolate.

Nearby is a stand of wind-gnarled poplars. From a limb hangs a beaten pair of binoculars. I examine this strange artifact, blinking back the hallucination of some wandering cave hunter leaving behind this priceless tool. But reality wades in. Silver Dollar is neither wilderness nor lost in time. Four decades ago my father hunted this far on foot. And later, as a teenager with my dog team, I did too. Men from the village twenty-five miles upriver frequently cross this lake on Yamaha,

Polaris, and Arctic Cat snowgos, searching for tracks, hunting the wolf packs and other furs and meat. Locally, the lake is known as the place to catch flightless geese during the molt. In summer when there is little else to hunt, a group of hunters occasionally will still walk this far.

Silver Dollar, to me, is simply a place where I feel awed, close to the land, close to home. My father used to snowshoe and walk the country a great deal. He could sense crossings where animals would pass. Good places to trap for furs. I never thought myself able to find such places. But in a way this lake is my crossing. I wander through life distressed by high technology coming to the Arctic, disabled by love for the land and animals and fear of development, people, and change. Yet, unconsciously, all my trails cross back here.

To the north sprawl the nameless mountains of the Brooks Range. Four miles west is my home. Migrating caribou crisscross this land, and now dollars do too. National park surrounds this place, begging for tourist statistics and appropriations; the Native corporation dreams strip mines and jobs and—somehow—subsistence hunting; the state schemes road corridors and petroleum. The oil companies have leap-frogged us and are galloping across the North slope, encircling us too, up the Chukchi coast. The bureaucrats have plans, big plans. For years I've struggled to write about this Arctic without telling a single secret, weaving between worry and worship, trying to say how much I care while hiding place names, all description that could lead a stranger to my priceless homeland. And meanwhile? We locals have woken up modern. Guidebooks leak misspelled seclusions to the Internet. *National Geographic* and Discovery Channel have come and gone. Disney, too. Paradoxically, now it seems I'm telling of this treasure in hopes of reminding us all to stand and guard our own.

I hang the old binocs back on the tree limb. Somehow—maybe it's these surroundings—I can't get away from the image of that long-ago mammoth hunter hanging the binoculars here. The three of us walk the tundra edge, peering down at water lapping under low caved-in permafrost banks. We spot no tusks curved like wrecked ship ribs. There is no shore, no beach with huge Flintstone bones lying about. There is no disappointment either. Being here outshines taking something from here. This I think we humans forget. In our first few million years we learned nothing about how not to hunger. We have no clue how not to take.

Even now the others are waiting, ready to head for home, and I find myself hunched over, wandering in small circles, searching for cranberries. I have to laugh, straighten up, and head across that tundra.

about the author

Seth Kantner was born and raised in the wilderness of northern Alaska. His debut novel, *Ordinary Wolves,* was a national bestseller and won the Pacific Northwest Booksellers Association Award and the Milkweed National Fiction Prize. His photography and writings have appeared in *Orion, Alaska*, the *New York Times, Prairie Schooner* and other publications. The recipient of a 2005 Whiting Writers' Award, Seth Kantner has also worked as a trapper, fisherman, mechanic, igloo builder, and wildlife photographer. He lives with his wife, Stacey, and daughter, China, in northwest Alaska.

acknowledgments

For stories and voices and ways of living on the land, I'd like to thank the Iñupiat—no one in particular, many old-timers dead and gone, many alive and well: your lives and food and customs in all their differences have surely shaped my life.

The Whiting Foundation folks, and the Rasmuson Foundation, gave me money that paid some bills and gave me time to write. Their respective support gave more than that—both explicitly encouraged me to stay with words.

My wife, Stacey, read and reread this manuscript, editing, organizing, and forming a structure out of my chaos. Sydelle Kramer, my agent far away in New York, sent a constant stream of wisdom and patience, putting up with my ability not to listen, throughout this project. My daughter, China, read every word, critiqued every photo, and always had handy a positive comment—and a bill for every cuss word.

Daniel Slager, Publisher of Milkweed Editions, foresaw what this book might be and gave me a contract for the manuscript in heap form. He and Publisher Emeritus Emilie Buchwald and Managing Director Hilary Reeves read and reread my work. Managing Editor James Cihlar edited this book and the thousand tiny details of the photos, and saw it through to the end. Thanks to all the staff at Milkweed for their kindness and for their belief in my work—in that order.

Dan O'Neill, fellow Alaskan writer, a man I'd never met at that time, read my pile of papers and provided editorial and historical advice, all while he was busy with his own work and on the Fourth of July; abstaining from a barbecue and drinks, he edited my entire book the day after I asked.

Nick Jans read my work and commented on my photos—in some cases camping with me, photographing—and as always was generous and humorous in his editing, his advice, and his sharing of his own experiences in the region.

My parents, Howard and Erna Kantner, and friends Don and Mary Williams and Keith and Anore Jones were more than helpful with stories and facts and photos, and in efforts to align my memories. That doesn't count the decades— thank you for those, too. And thanks to my mom for my first Nikon camera and lenses.

Thanks to the people who write to me and ask for the past, to Greg Garrett for ten words, and to Larry Kaplan, a genius at Iñupiaq, for a dozen more. Thanks to those I'm forgetting right now—another talent of mine. And, again to Stacey, and Sydelle: without your support and help I would wander back to being a trapper or a sled maker.

Material from this book, in somewhat similar form, previously appeared in the following publications. Thanks to the editors and publishers who printed my work:

"Bob and Carrie Come out of the Hills" first appeared in the *Anchorage Daily News*.

"Creature from the Ice Age" ("Hanging Out with the Hang-out Kings") first appeared in a very different form in *Ruralite* in April 2003.

"Flower of the Fringe" first appeared in *Orion* in December 2005.

"Good-bye Our Season" first appeared in *Alaska* in February 1997 and later in *Switch!* (Japan) in December 1998.

"Ice Fishing" ("Counting Fish") first appeared in a different form in *Alaska Geographic*, volume 27, number 4, 2000.

"My Alaska" ("Silver Strangers") first appeared in *Fish Alaska* in February 2007.

"Salting a Moose" first appeared in different form in the *Anchorage Daily News*.

"Shopping for Porcupine" first appeared in *Alaska* in October 1999.

"Susan's Candy Store" ("The Candy Store") first appeared in *Alaska Quarterly Review* in Spring/Summer 2007.

"The Hunter" ("Iñupiaq Mailman") first appeared in *Outside* in February 1995.

"Trapping with Dogs" ("Brothers on the Trapline") first appeared in a different form in *Alaska Geographic*, volume 27, number 4, 2000.

More Nonfiction Books from Milkweed Editions

To order books or for more information, contact Milkweed at
(800) 520-6455
or visit our Web site (www.milkweed.org).

Postcards from Ed:
Dispatches and Salvos from an
American Iconoclast
Ed Abbey
Edited and Introduced by
David Petersen

Toward the Livable City
Edited by Emilie Buchwald

Boundary Waters:
The Grace of the Wild
Paul Gruchow

Grass Roots:
The Universe of Home
Paul Gruchow

The Future of Nature:
Writing on a Human Ecology from
Orion *Magazine*
Selected by Barry Lopez

Hope, Human and Wild: True Stories
of Living Lightly on the Earth
Bill McKibben

The Pine Island Paradox
Kathleen Dean Moore

The Barn at the End of the World:
The Apprenticeship of a Quaker,
Buddhist Shepherd
Mary Rose O'Reilley

The Love of Impermanent Things:
A Threshold Ecology
Mary Rose O'Reilley

North to Katahdin
Eric Pinder

Ecology of a Cracker Childhood
Janisse Ray

The Wet Collection
Joni Tevis

Milkweed Editions

Founded in 1979, Milkweed Editions is one of the largest independent, non-profit literary publishers in the United States. Milkweed publishes with the intention of making a humane impact on society, in the belief that good writing can transform the human heart and spirit. Within this mission, Milkweed publishes in four areas: fiction, nonfiction, poetry, and children's literature for middle-grade readers.

Join Us

Milkweed depends on the generosity of foundations and individuals like you, in addition to the sales of its books. In an increasingly consolidated and bottom-line-driven publishing world, your support allows us to select and publish books on the basis of their literary quality and the depth of their message. Please visit our Web site (www.milkweed.org) or contact us at (800) 520-6455 to learn more about our donor program.

Interior design by Linda McKnight
Typesetting by Blue Heron Typesetters
Typeset in Sabon and Gill Sans
Printed on acid-free paper
by Friesens Corporation.